Real World

Colouring Book

For Advanced Users & Adults

50 Images

Created From Real Life Photos
For You To Colour As You Please.

ISBN 978-0-359-93594-9

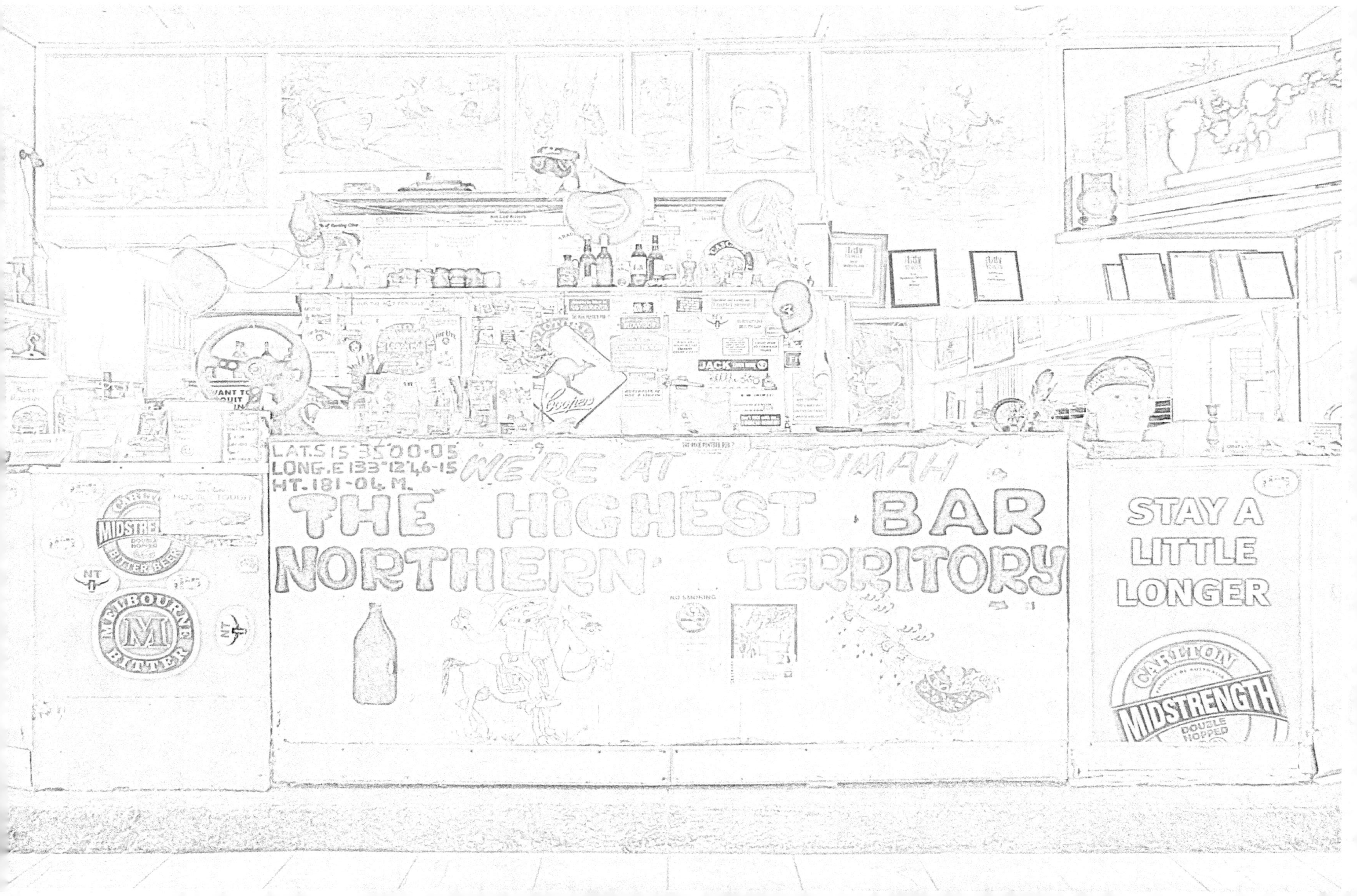

LAT.S15 35'00-05
LONG.E133 12'4,6-15
HT.181-04.M.
WE'RE AT LARRIMAH
"THE" HIGHEST BAR
NORTHERN TERRITORY
NO SMOKING
STAY A
LITTLE
LONGER
CARLTON
MIDSTRENGTH
DOUBLE HOPPED
MELBOURNE BITTER
NT
Coopers

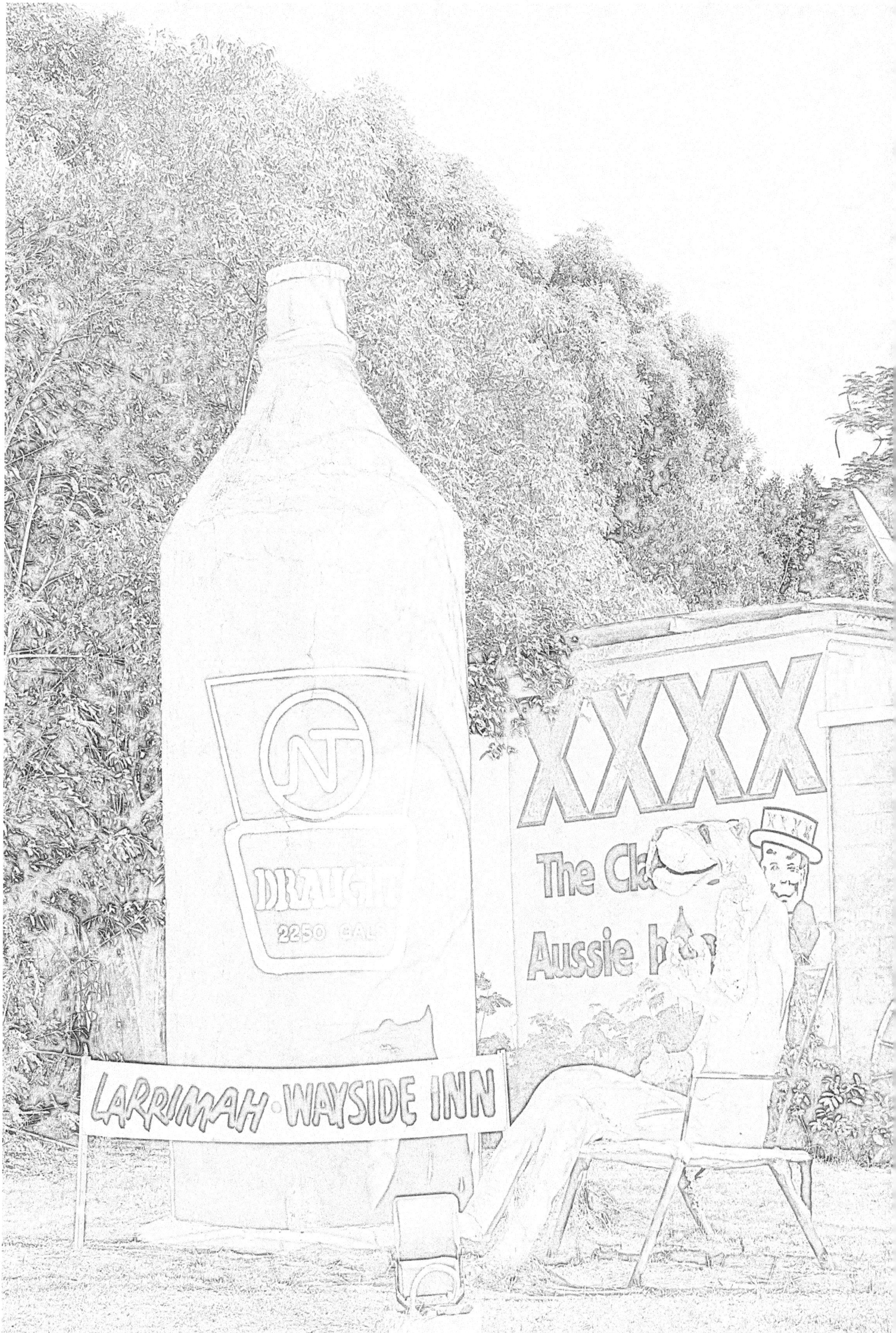
XXXX
LARRIMAH · WAYSIDE INN

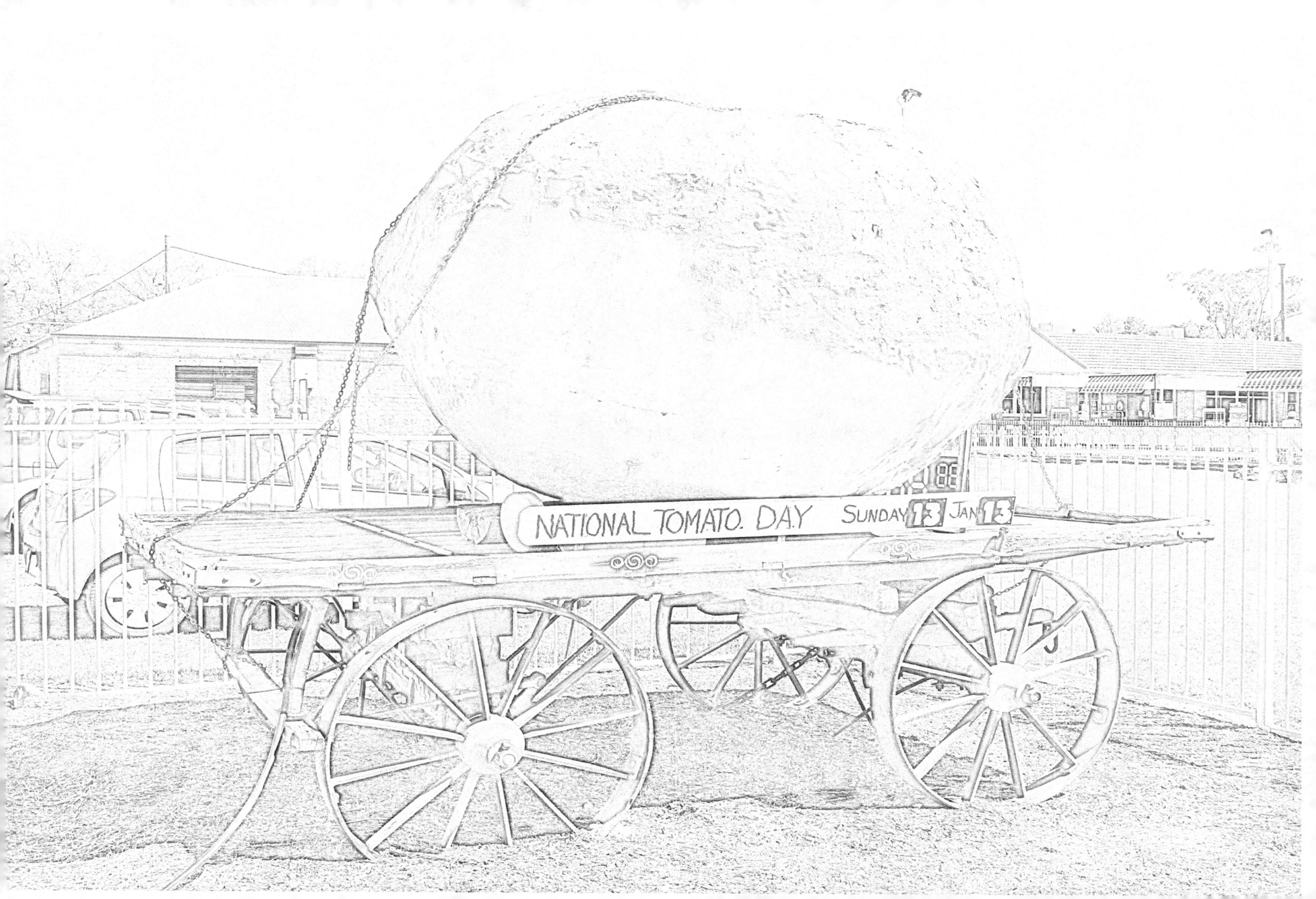
NATIONAL TOMATO. DAY
SUNDAY 13 JAN 13

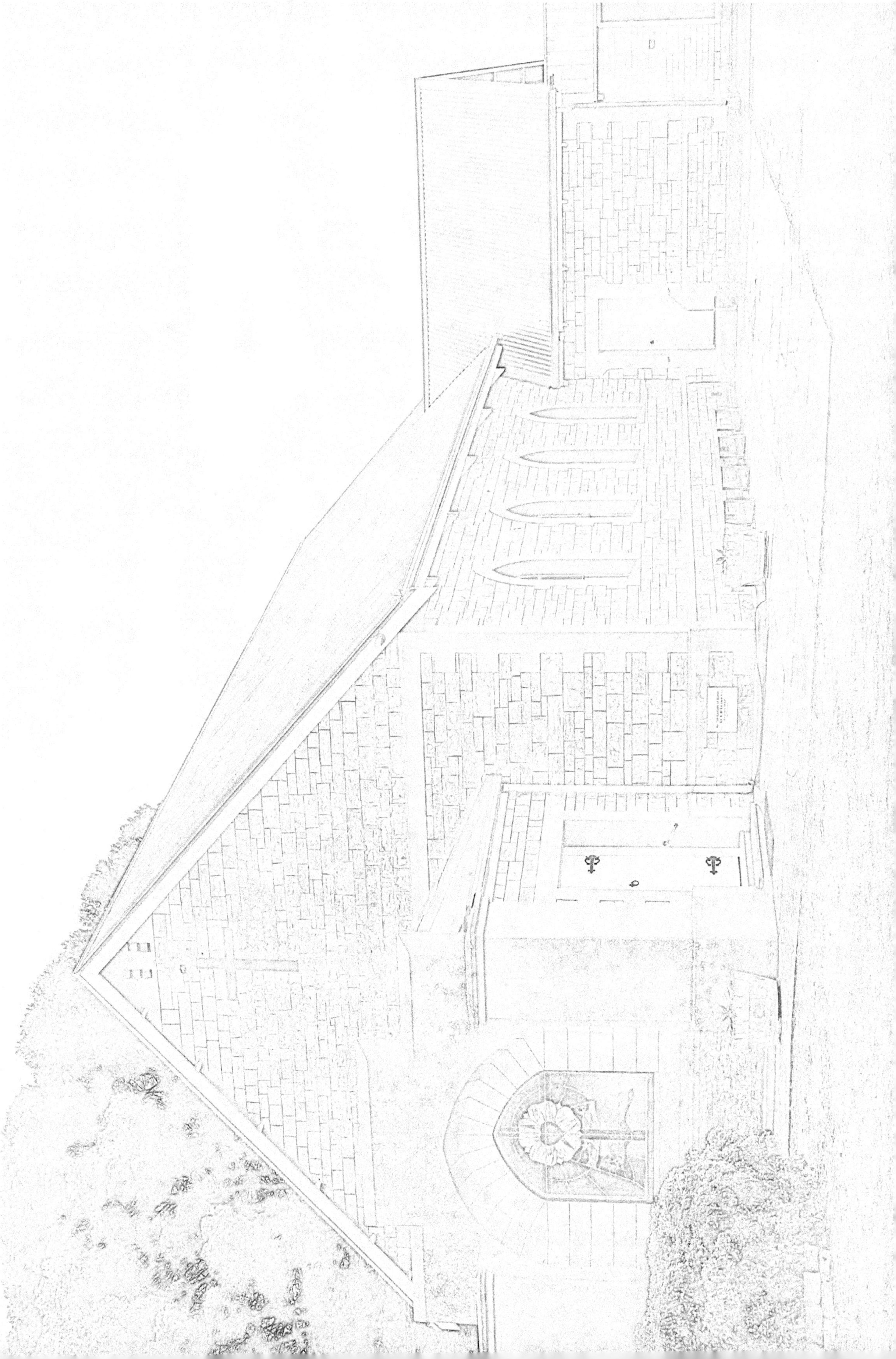

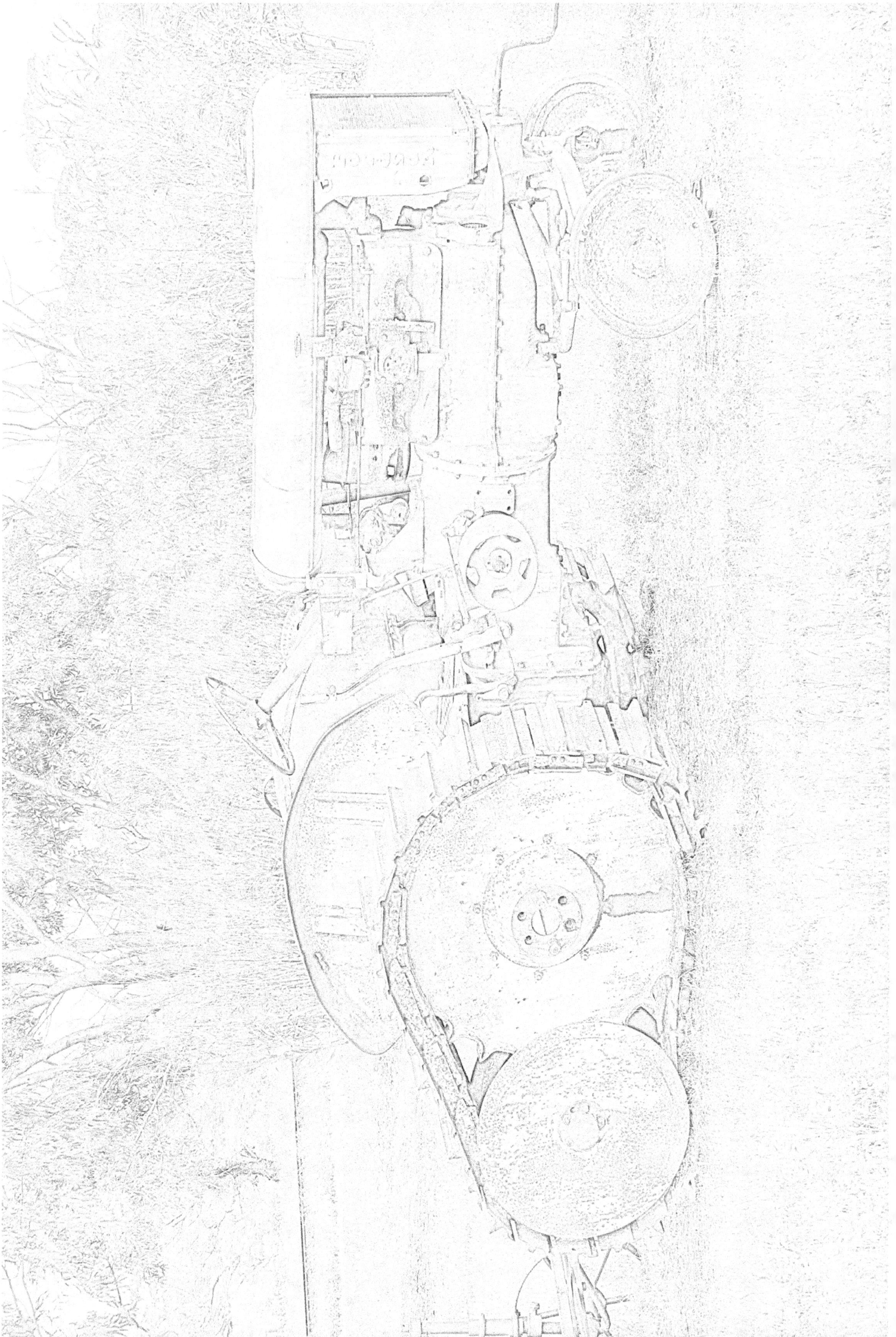

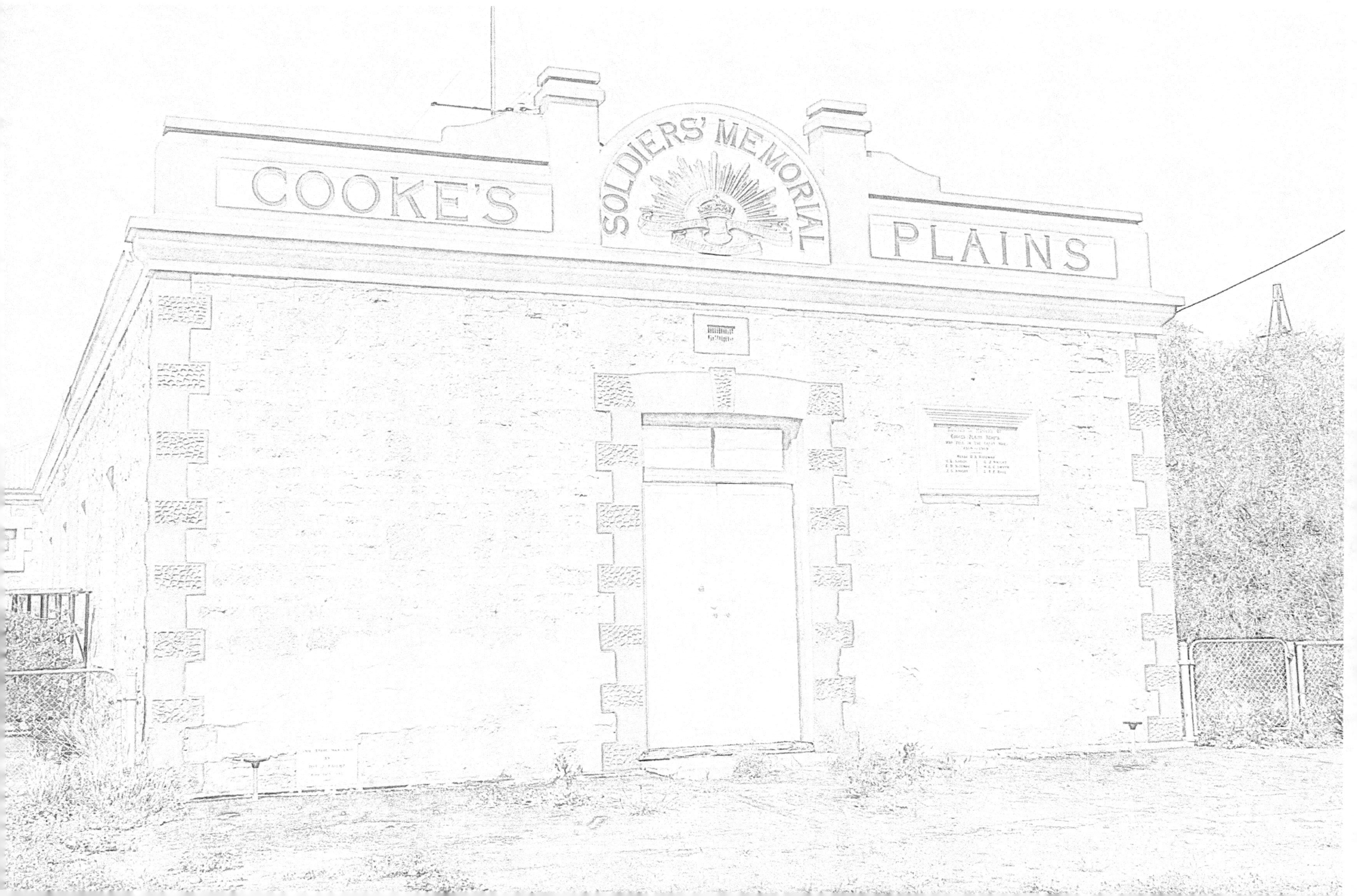
COOKE'S
SOLDIERS' MEMORIAL
PLAINS

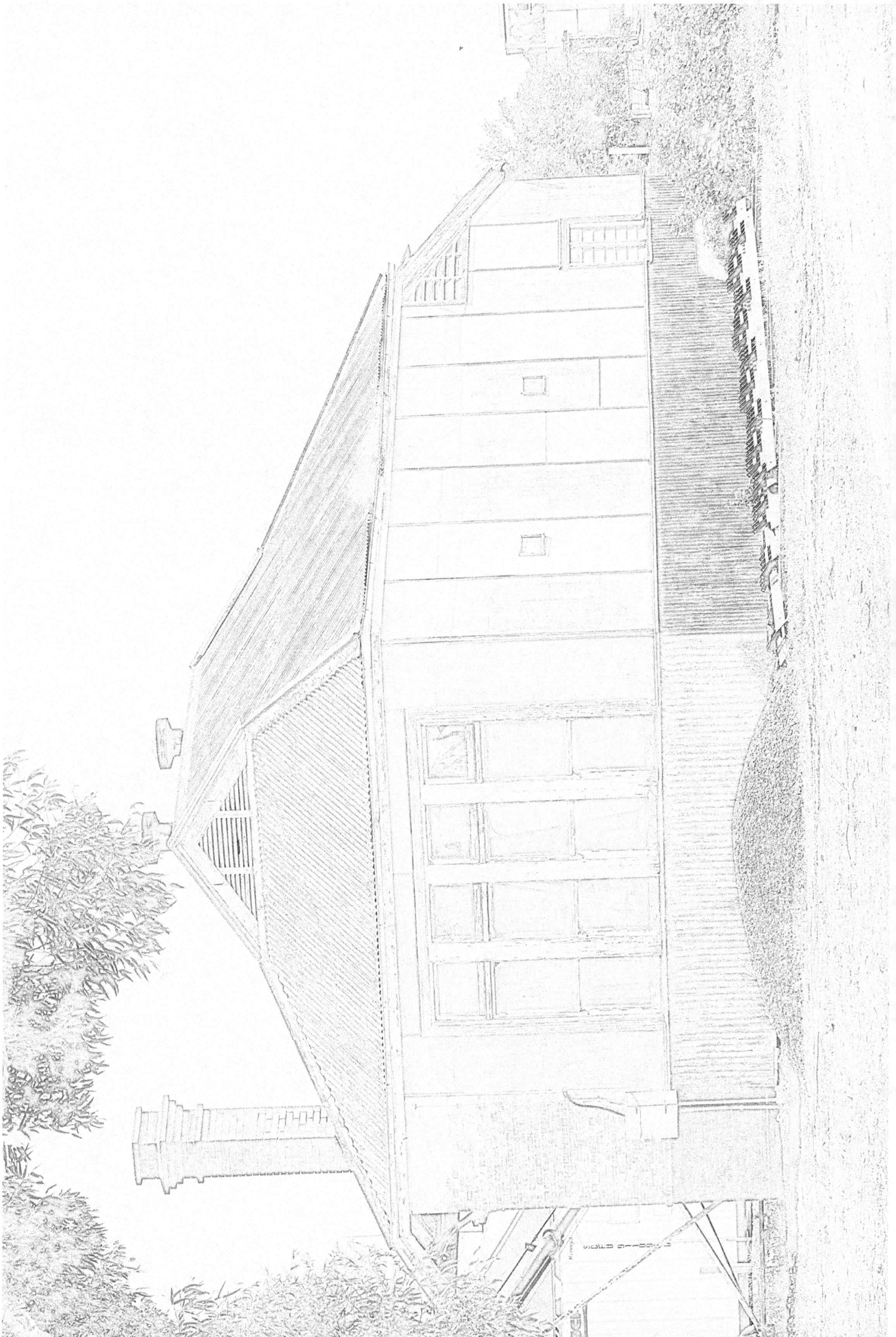

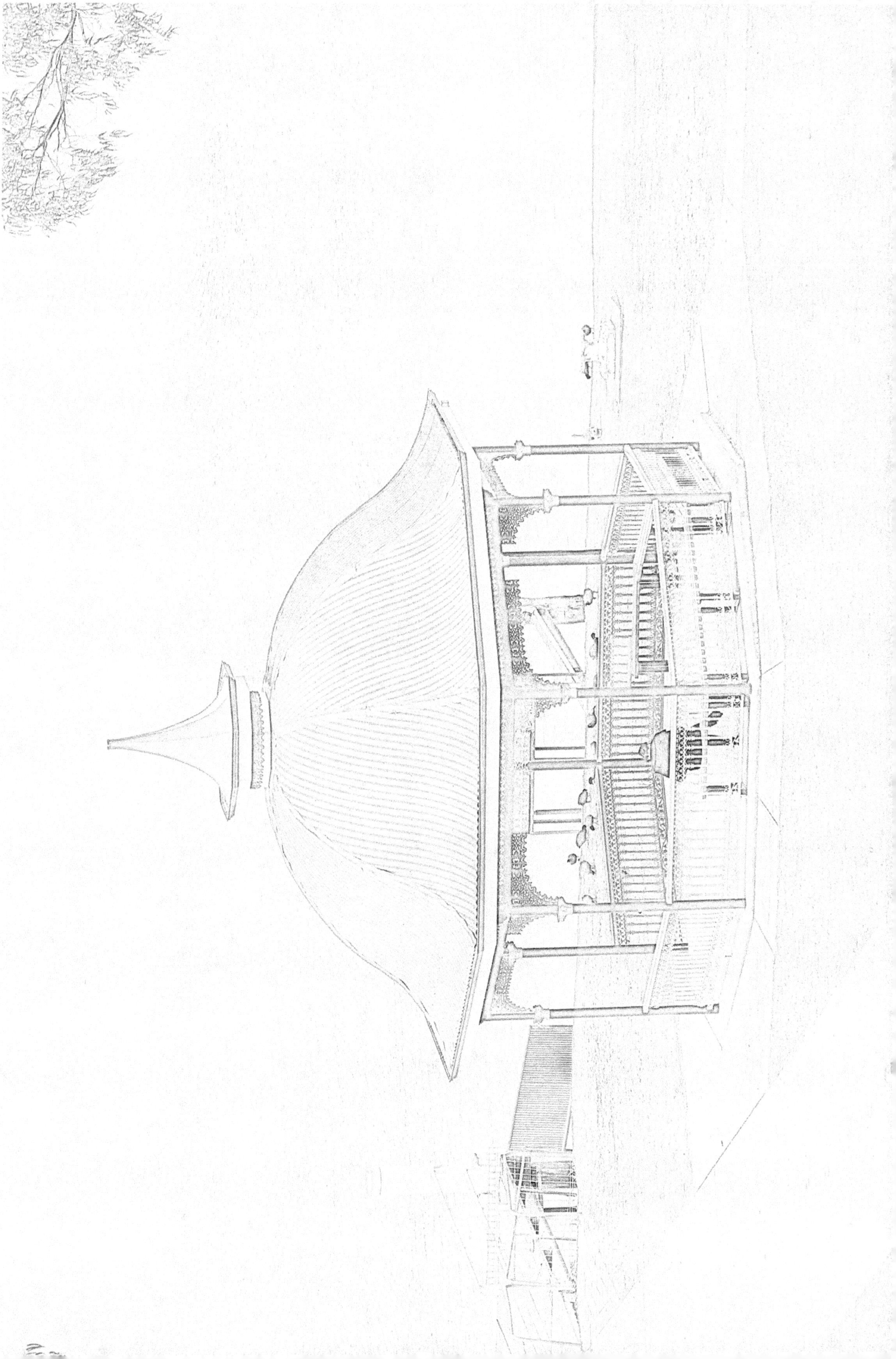

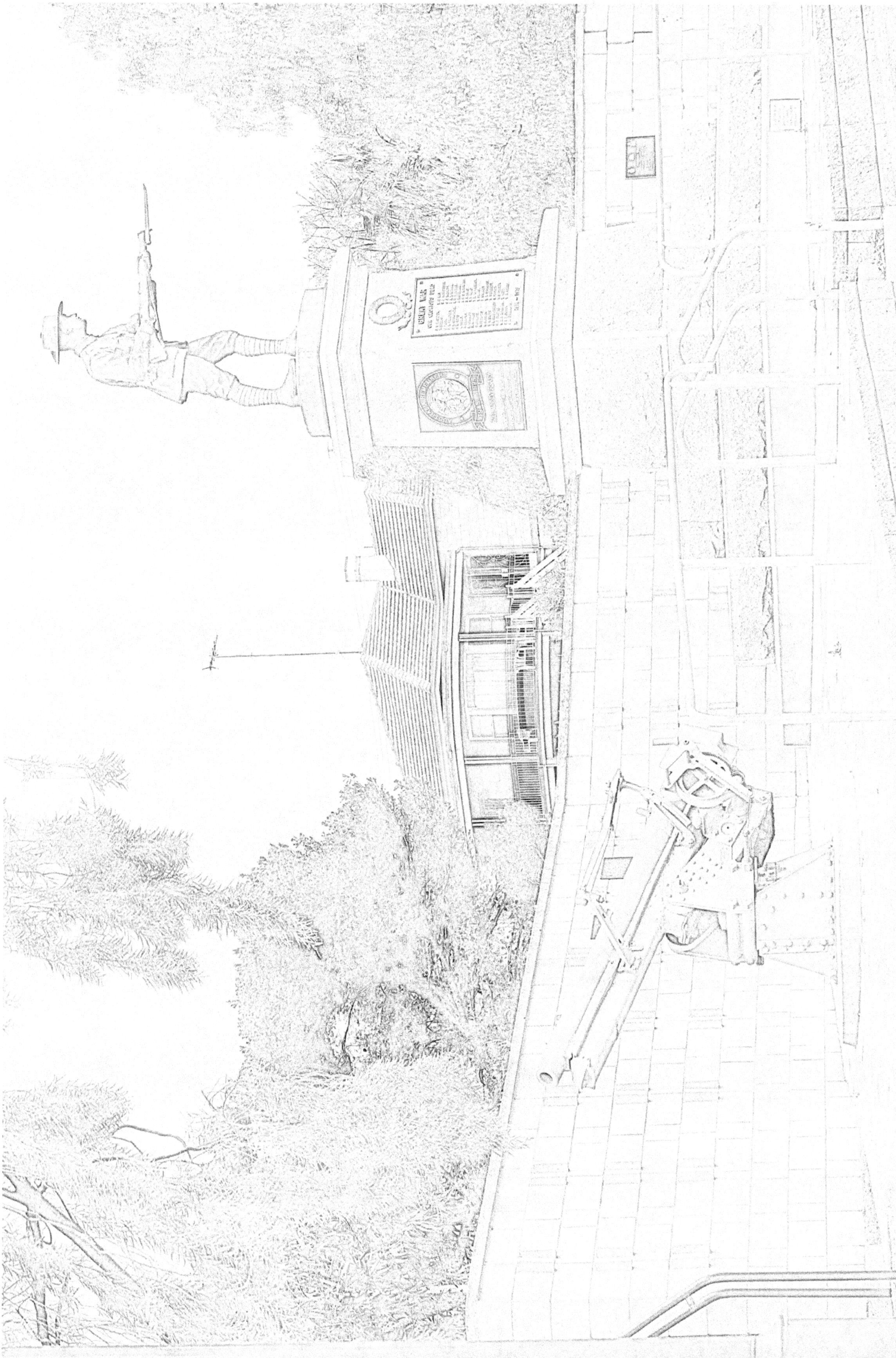

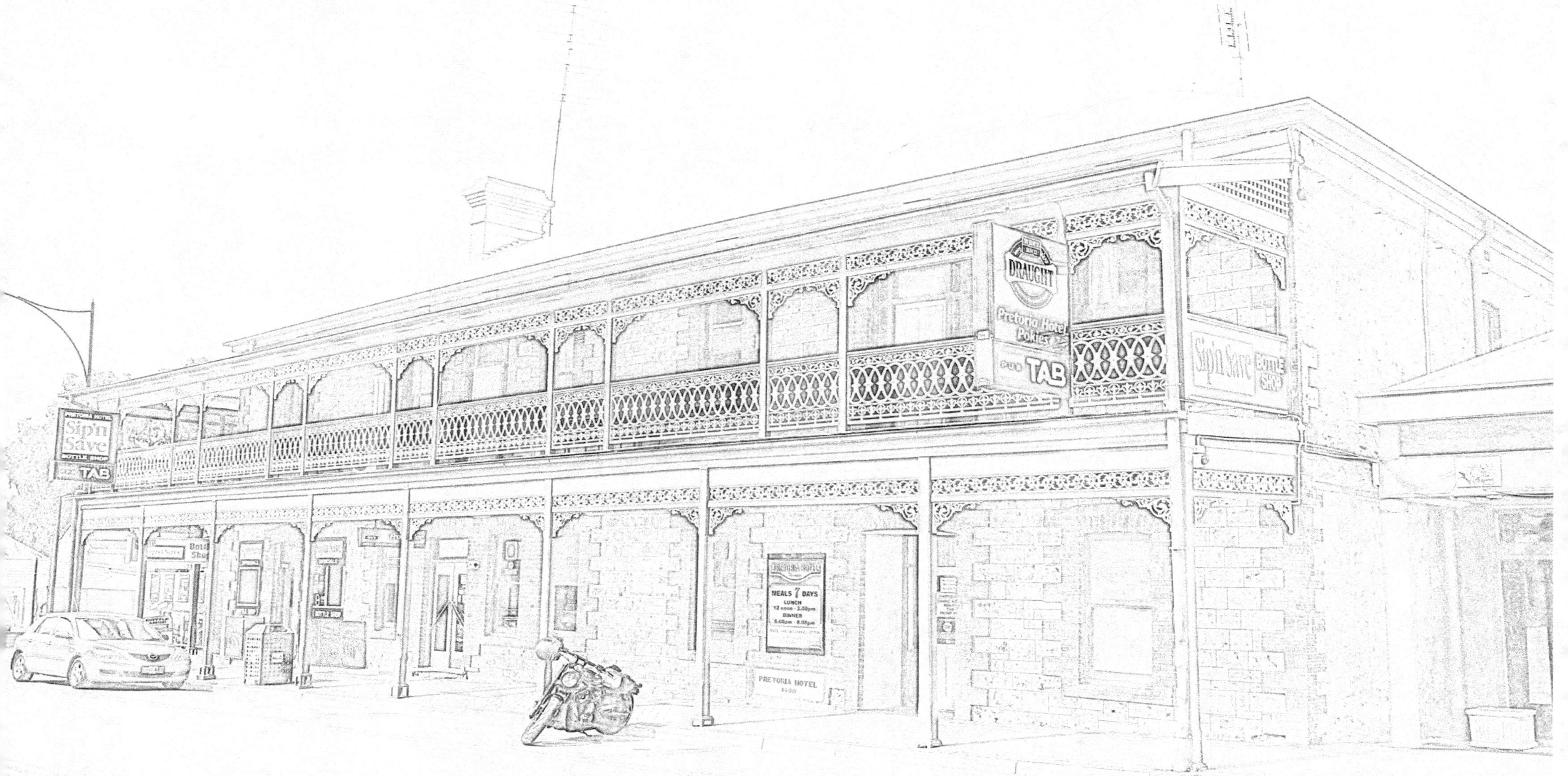
DRAUGHT
Pretoria Hotel
Pokies
PUB TAB
Sip'n Save
BOTTLE SHOP
PRETORIA HOTEL
Sip'n Save
BOTTLE SHOP
TAB
PRETORIA HOTEL
MEALS 7 DAYS
LUNCH
12 noon - 2.00pm
DINNER
6.00pm - 8.00pm
PRETORIA HOTEL

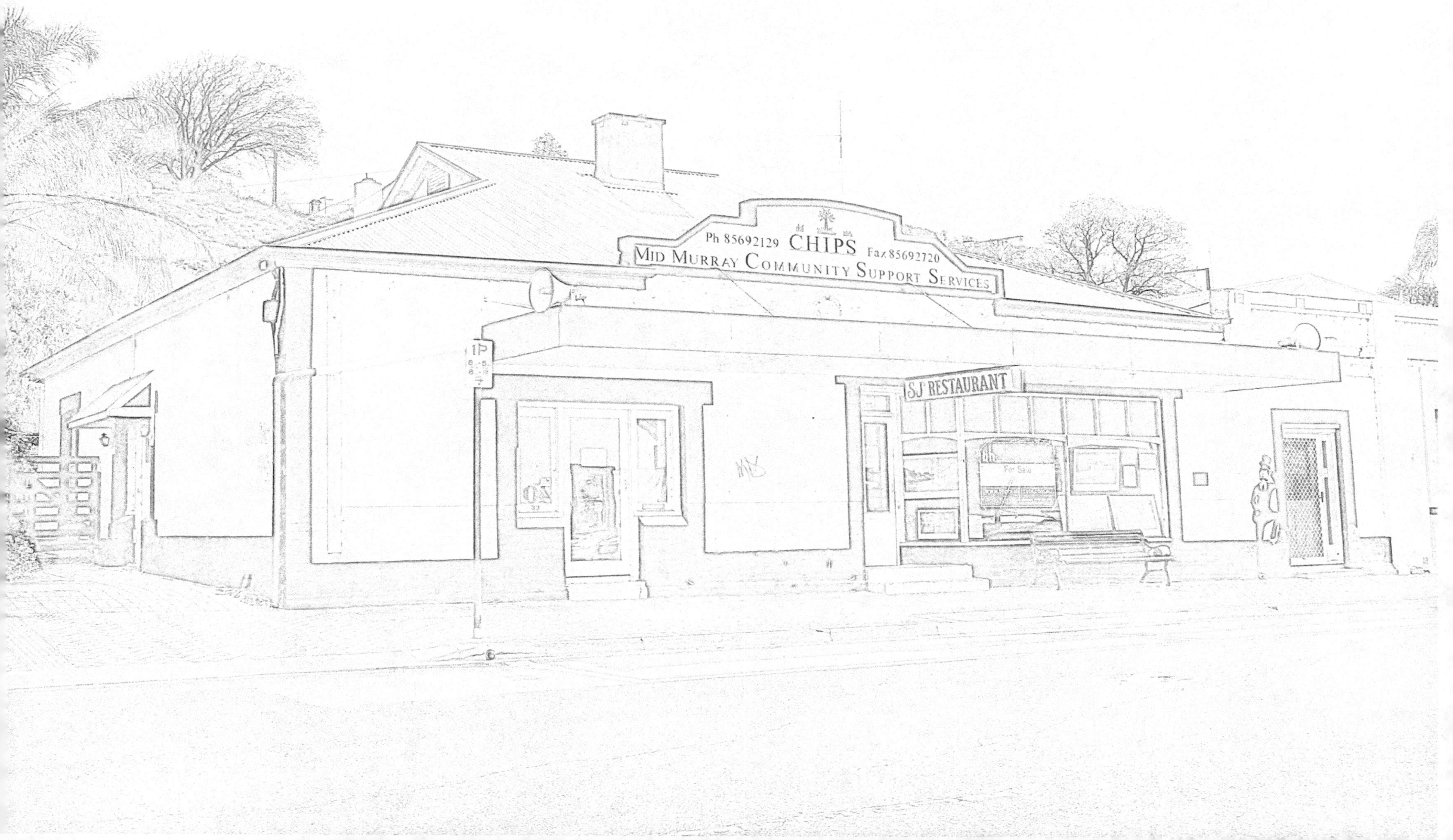
Ph 85692129 CHIPS Fax 85692720
MID MURRAY COMMUNITY SUPPORT SERVICES
SJ RESTAURANT
1P

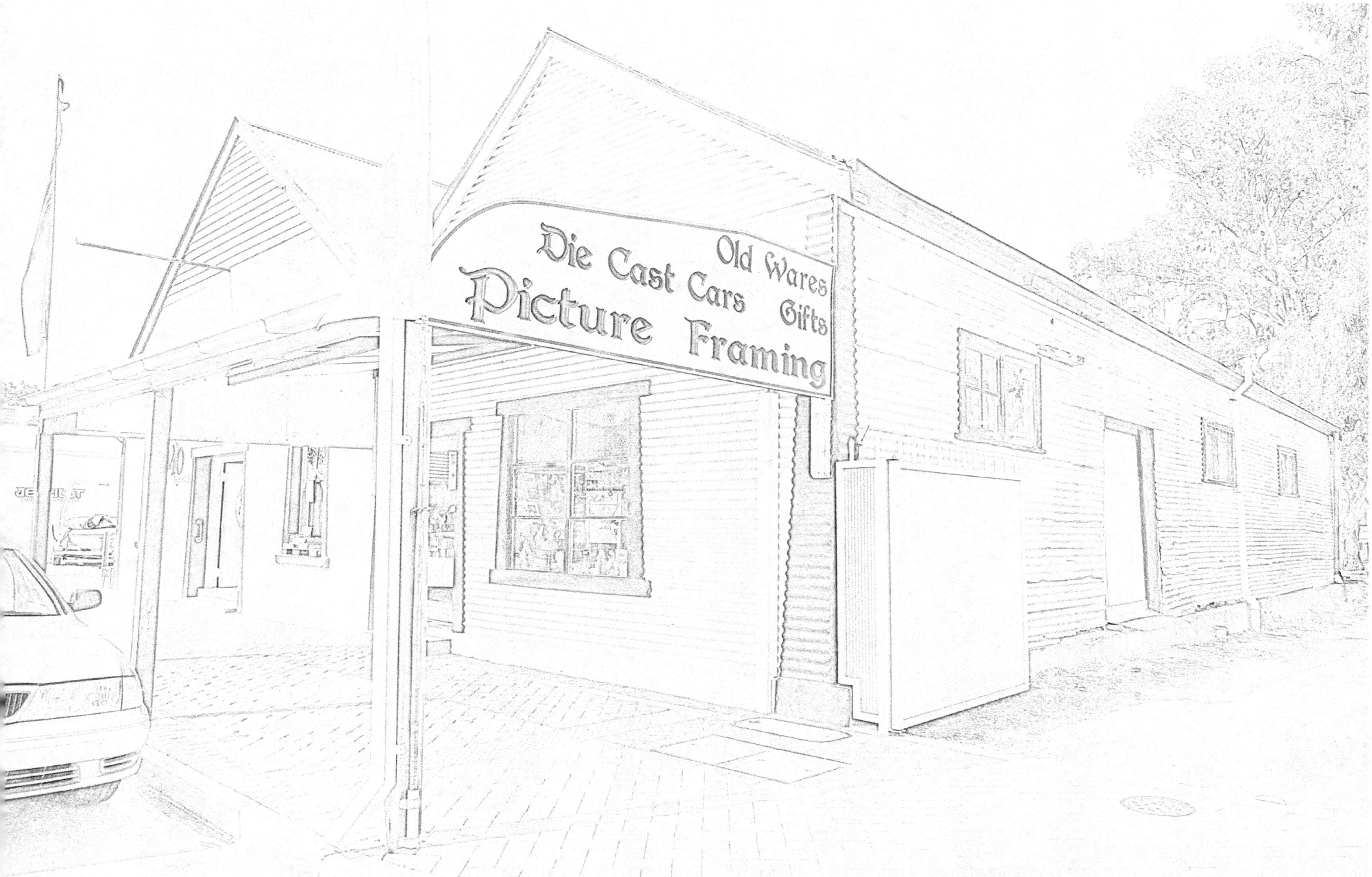

Old Wares
Die Cast Cars
Gifts
Picture Framing

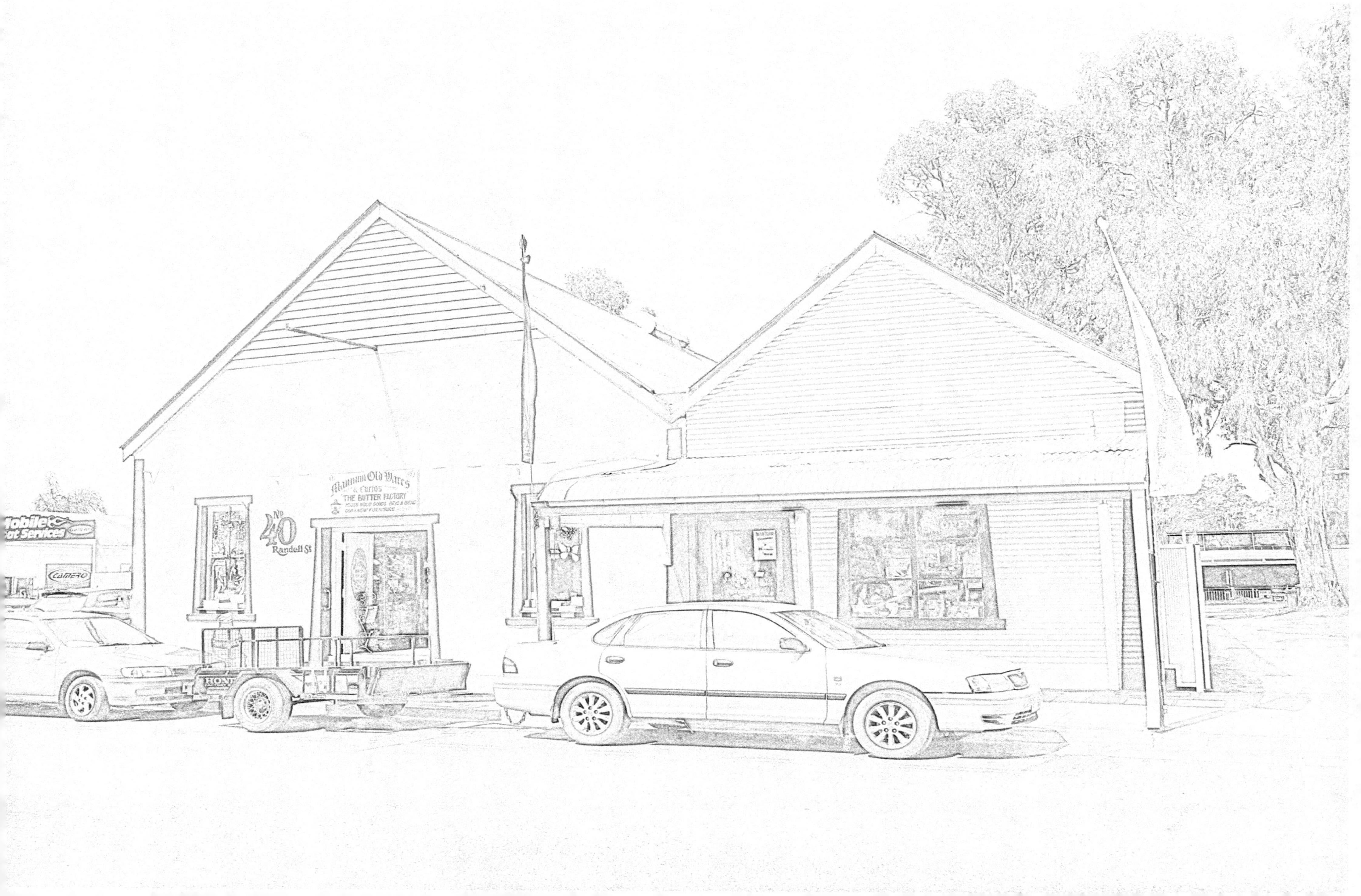
Mannum Old Wares
& Curios
THE BUTTER FACTORY
No 40
Randell St
CAMERO

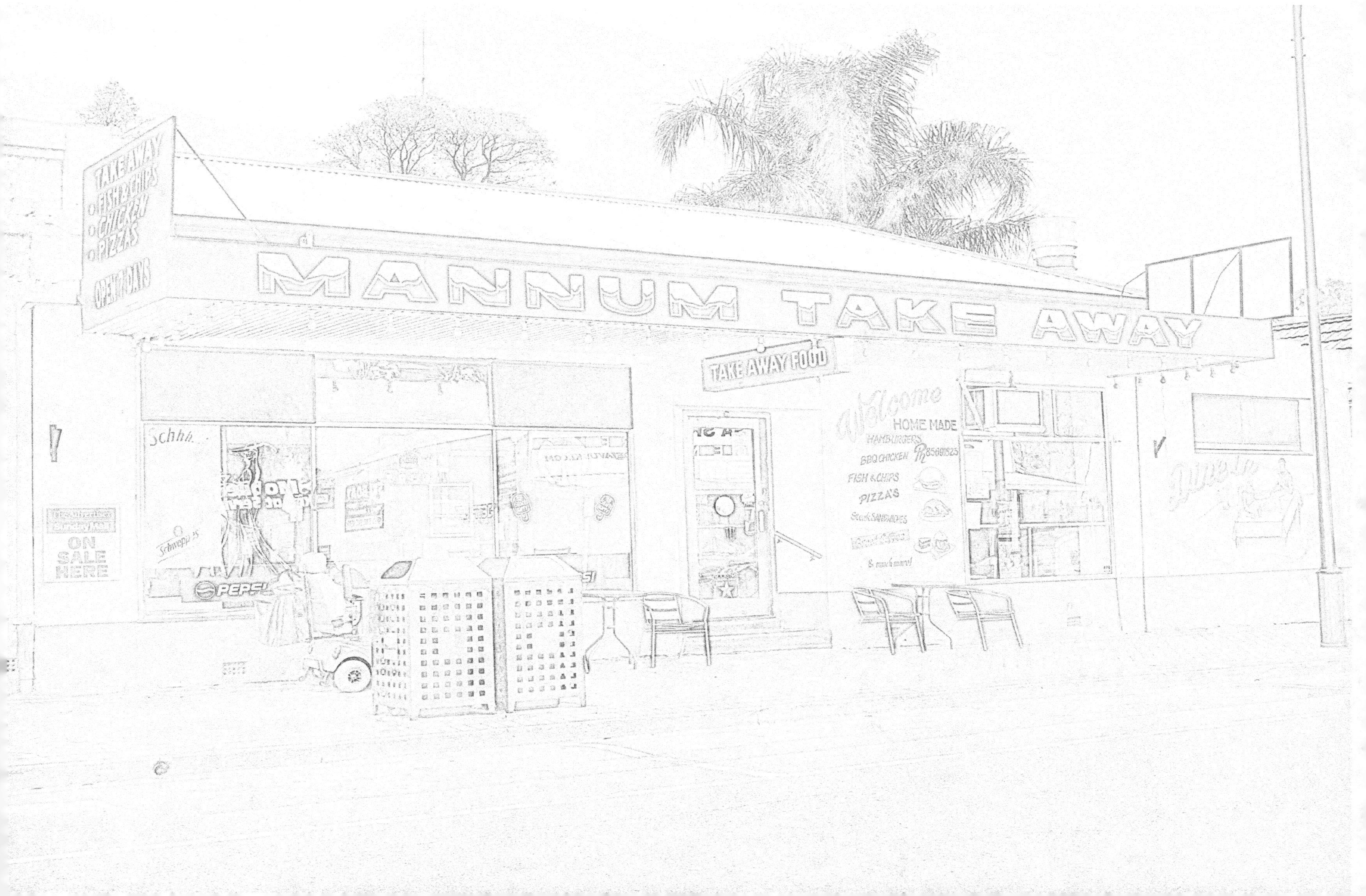
TAKE AWAY
FISH & CHIPS
CHICKEN
PIZZAS
OPEN 7 DAYS
MANNUM TAKE AWAY
TAKE AWAY FOOD
Welcome
HOME MADE
HAMBURGERS
BBQ CHICKEN
Ph 85691825
FISH & CHIPS
PIZZA'S
Steak SANDWICHES
& much more!
Schhh...
Schweppes
PEPSI
ON SALE HERE

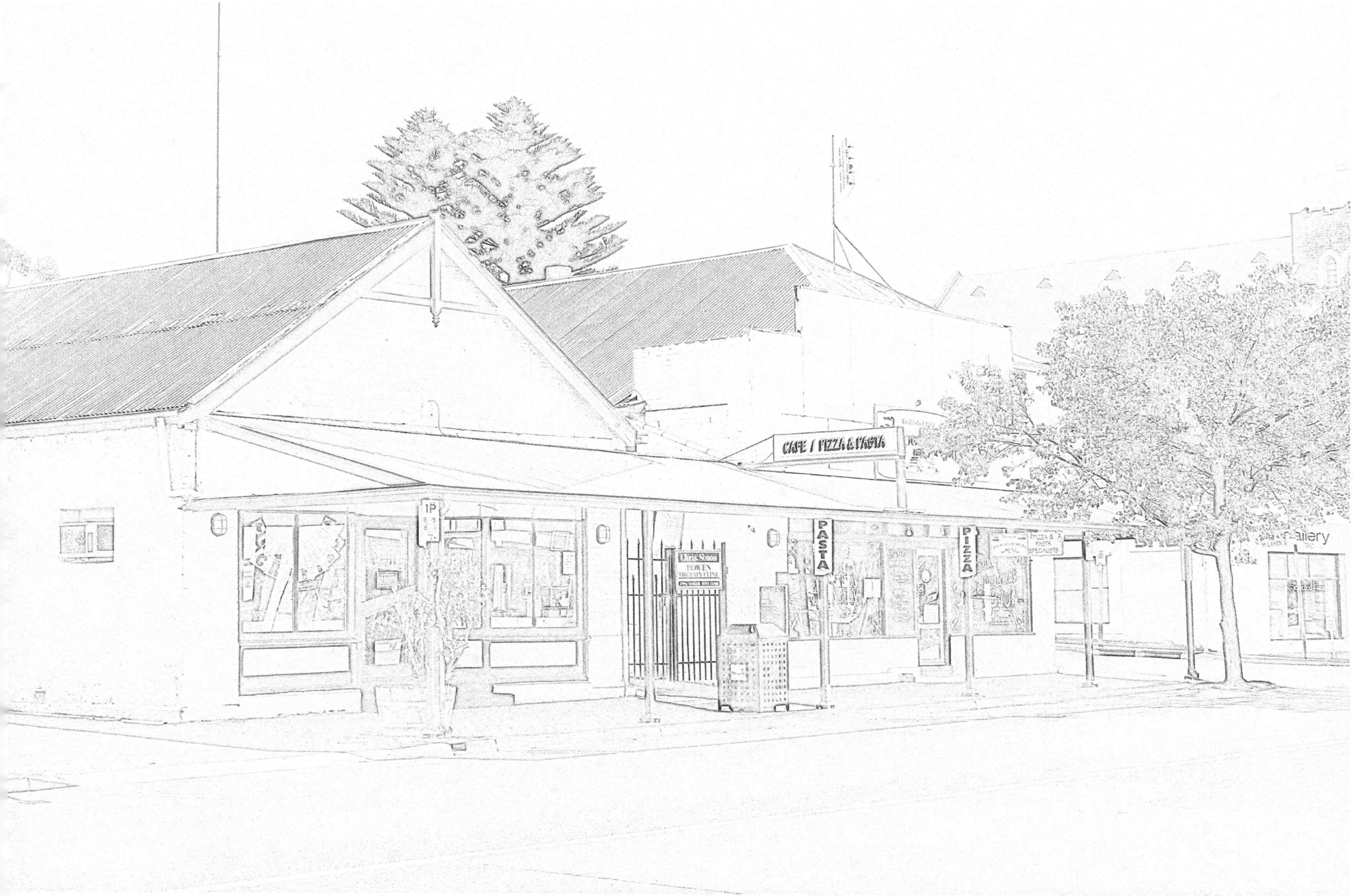
CAFE / PIZZA & PASTA
1P
PASTA
PIZZA
PIZZA & PASTA SPECIALISTS
BOWEN THERAPY CLINIC
Gallery

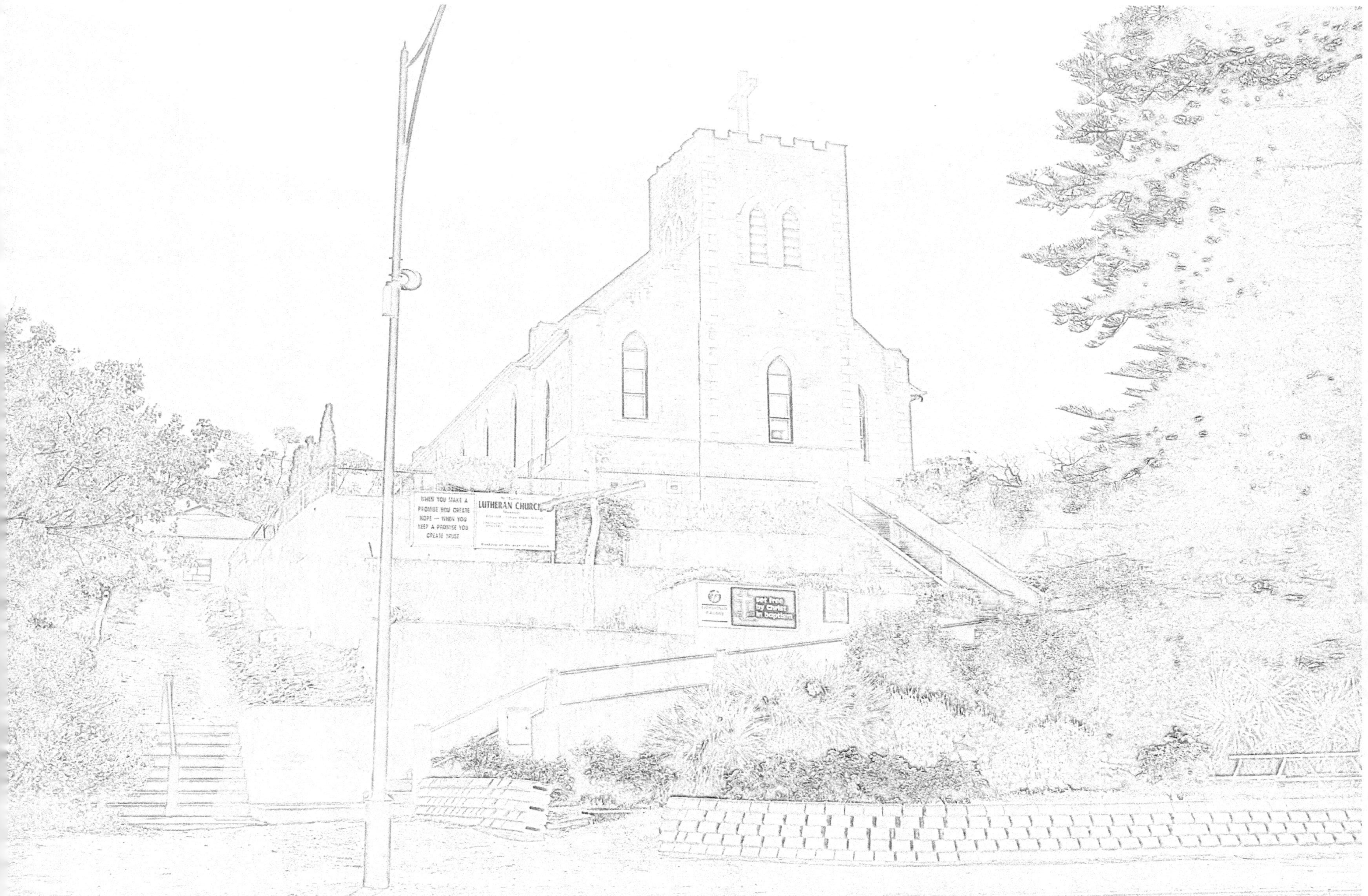
WHEN YOU MAKE A
PROMISE YOU CREATE
HOPE — WHEN YOU
KEEP A PROMISE YOU
CREATE TRUST
LUTHERAN CHURCH
set free
by Christ
in baptism

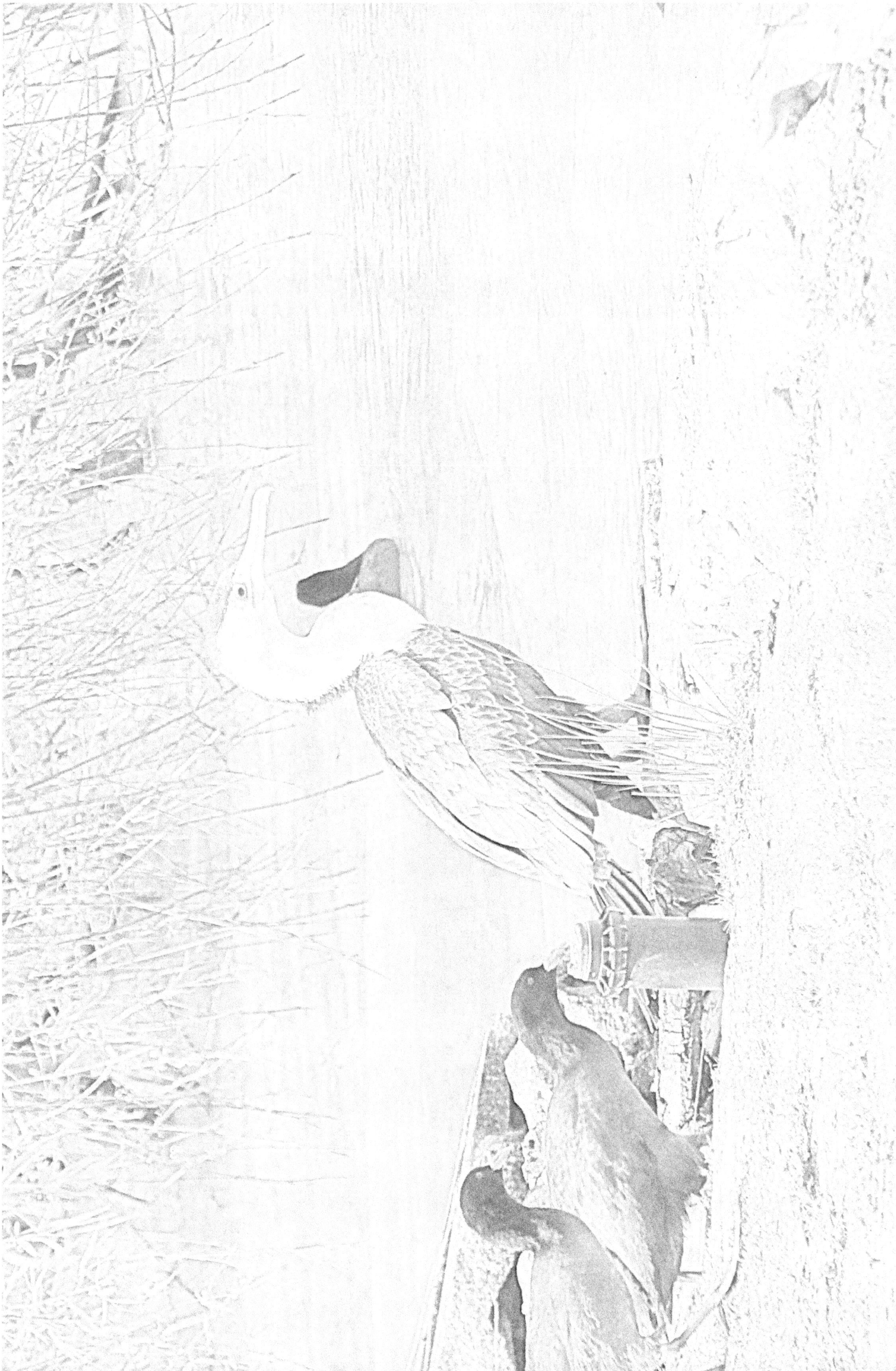

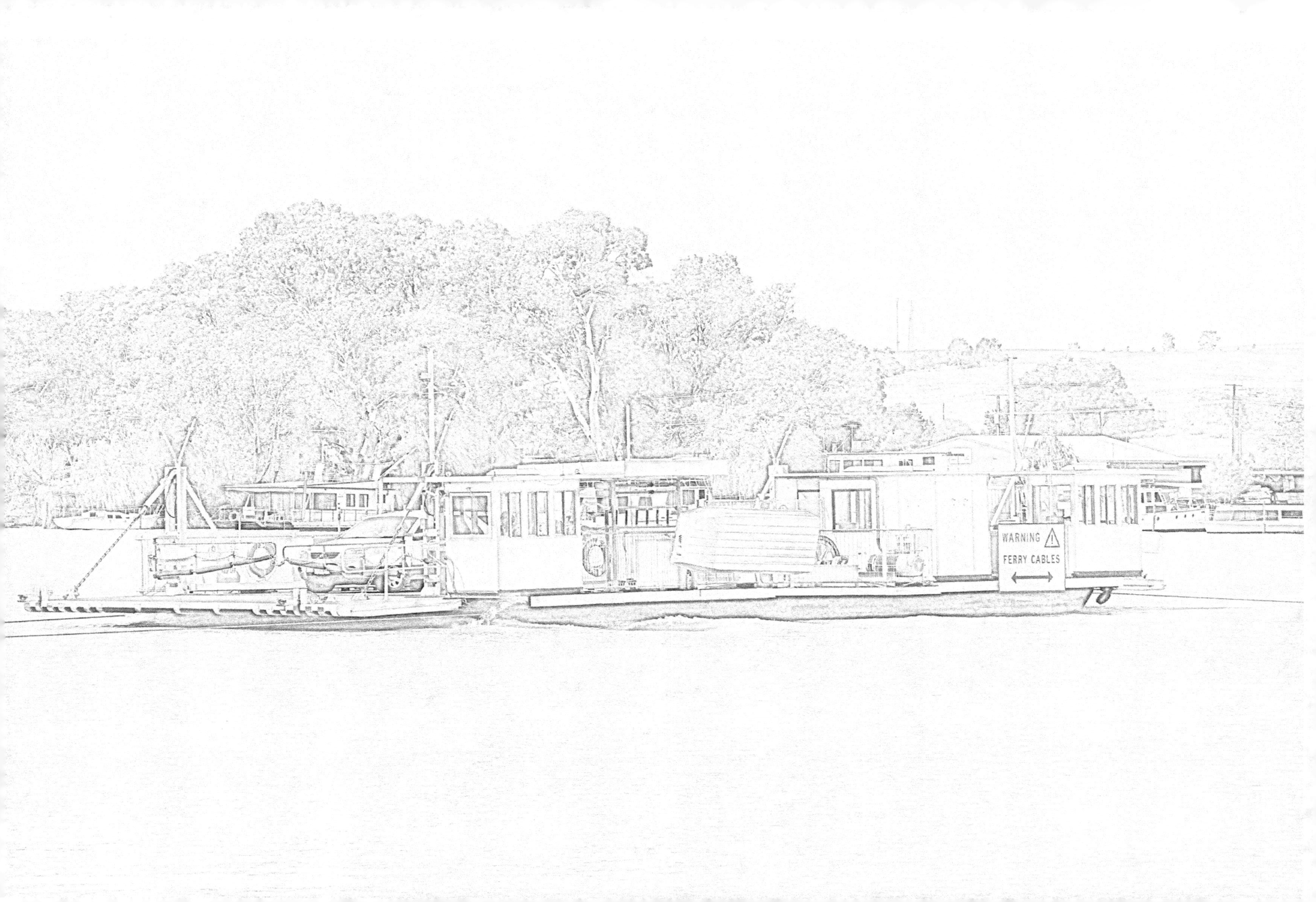
WARNING
FERRY CABLES

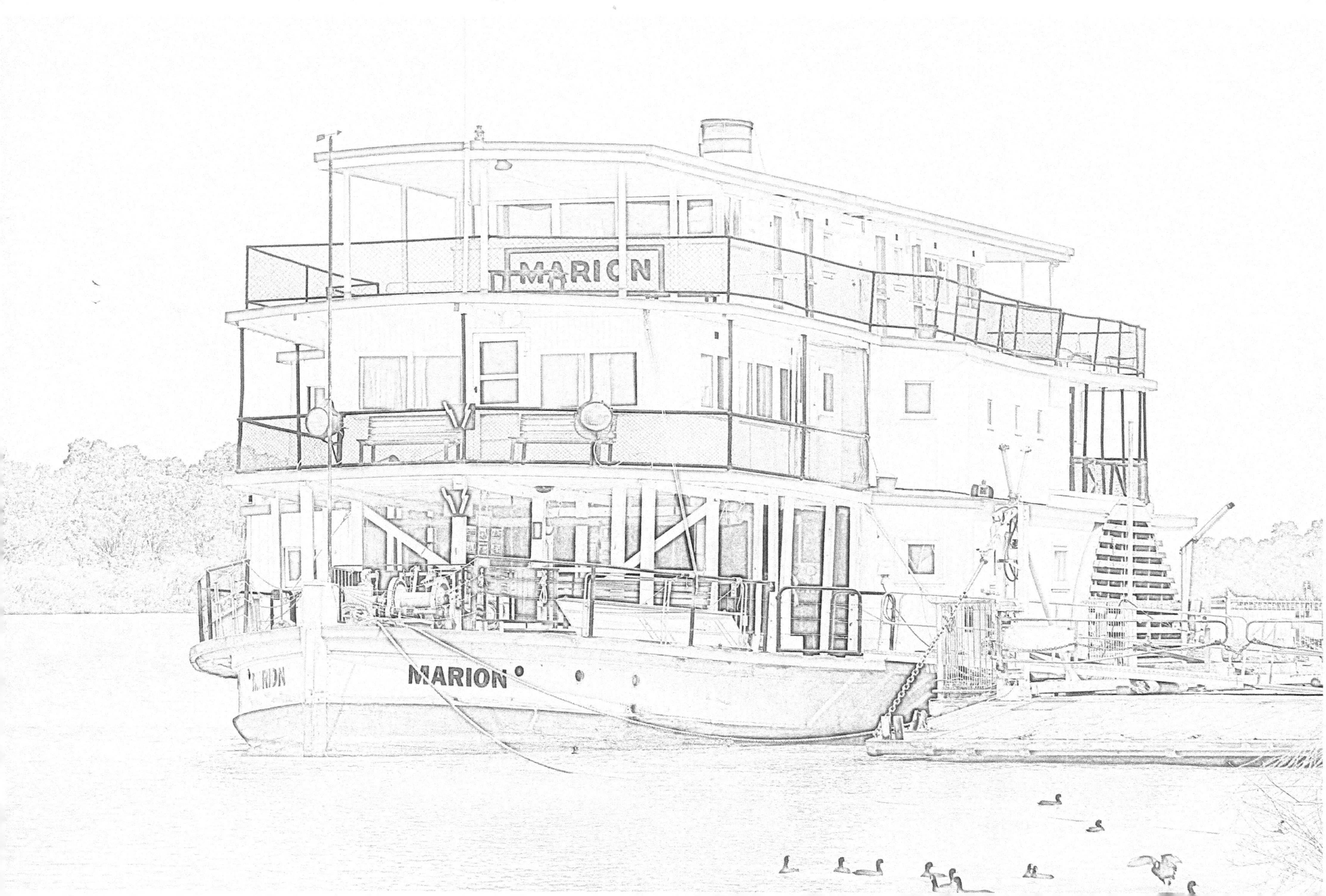
MARION
MARION

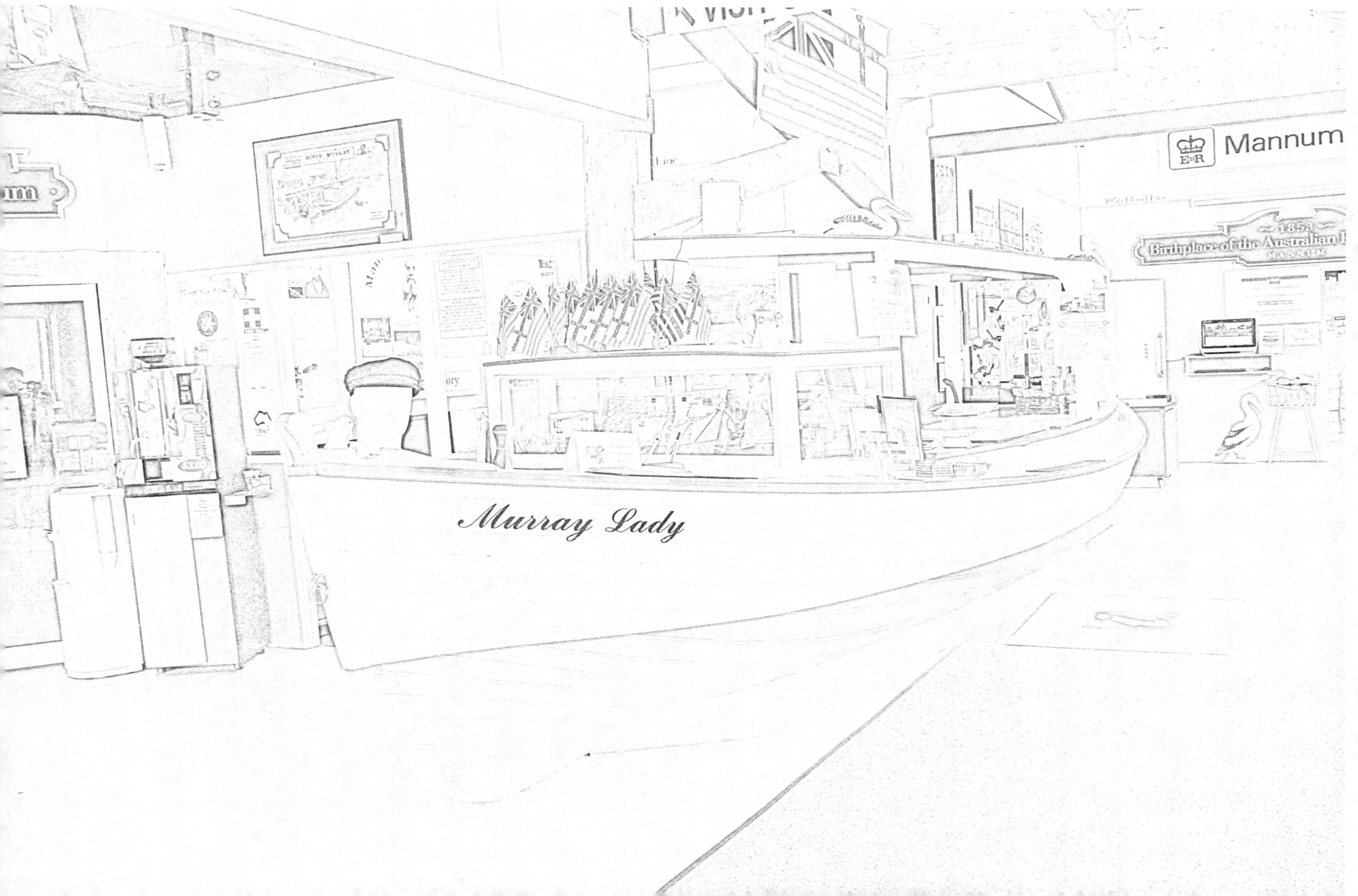
Mannum
1853
Birthplace of the Australian
MANNUM
Murray Lady

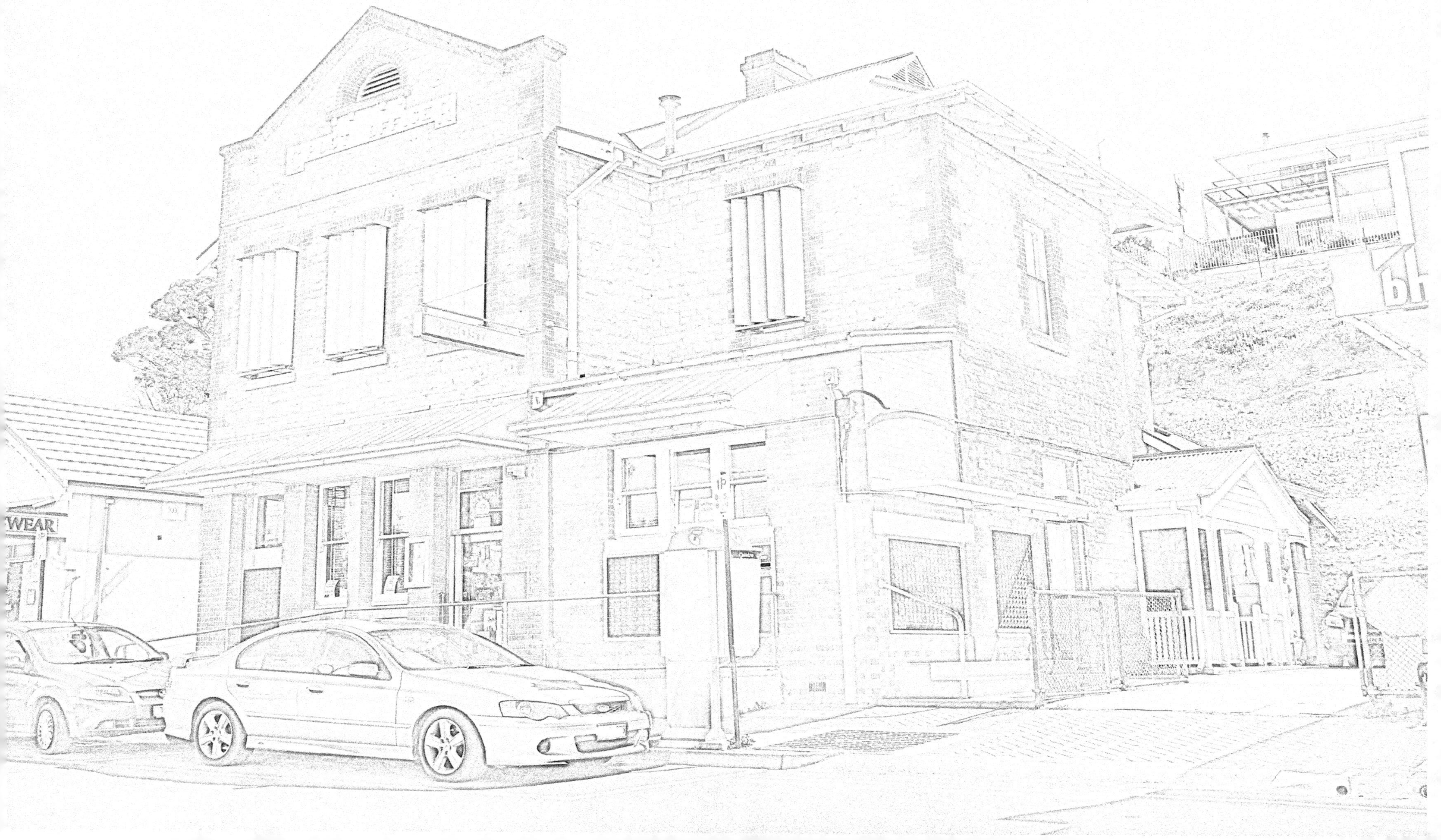
WEAR

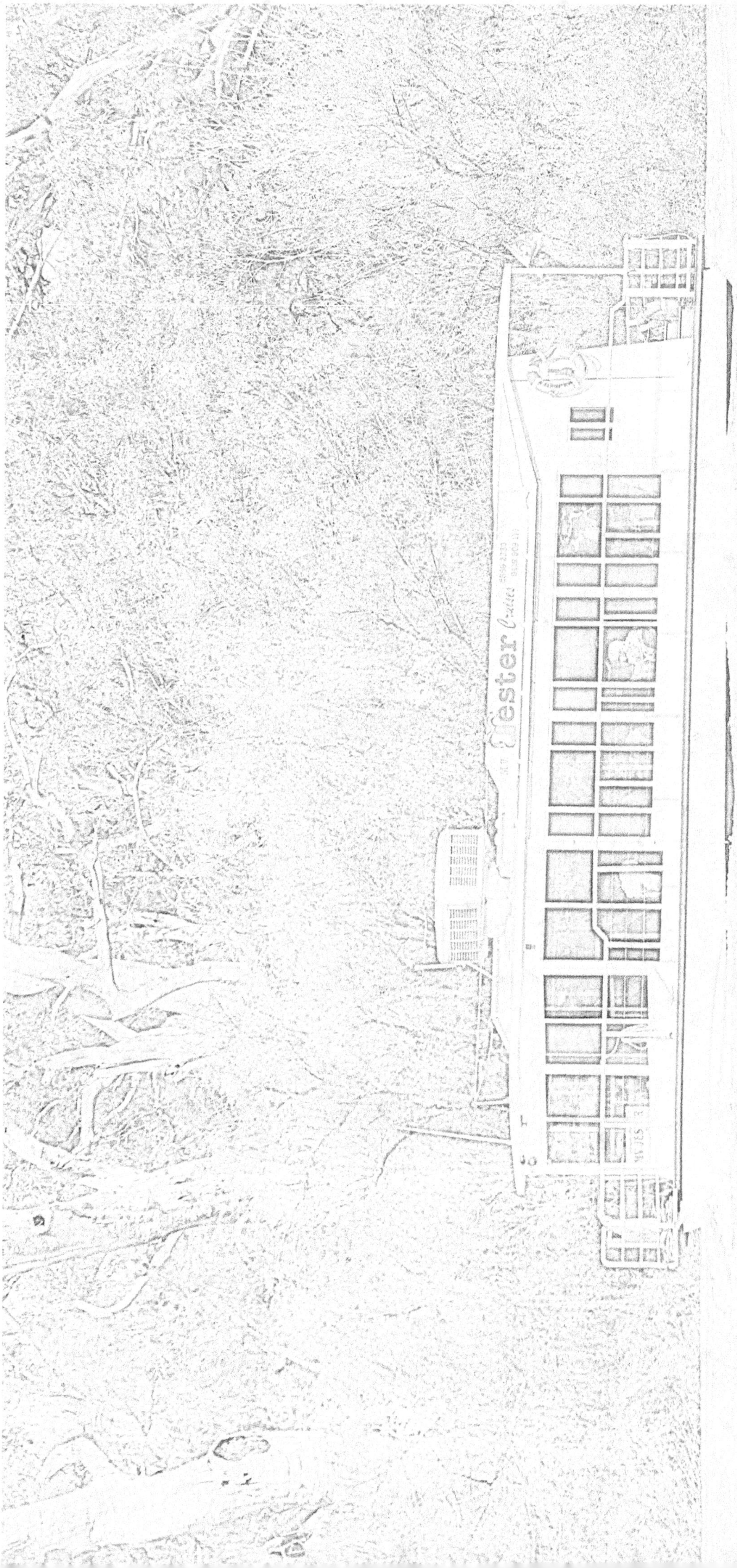

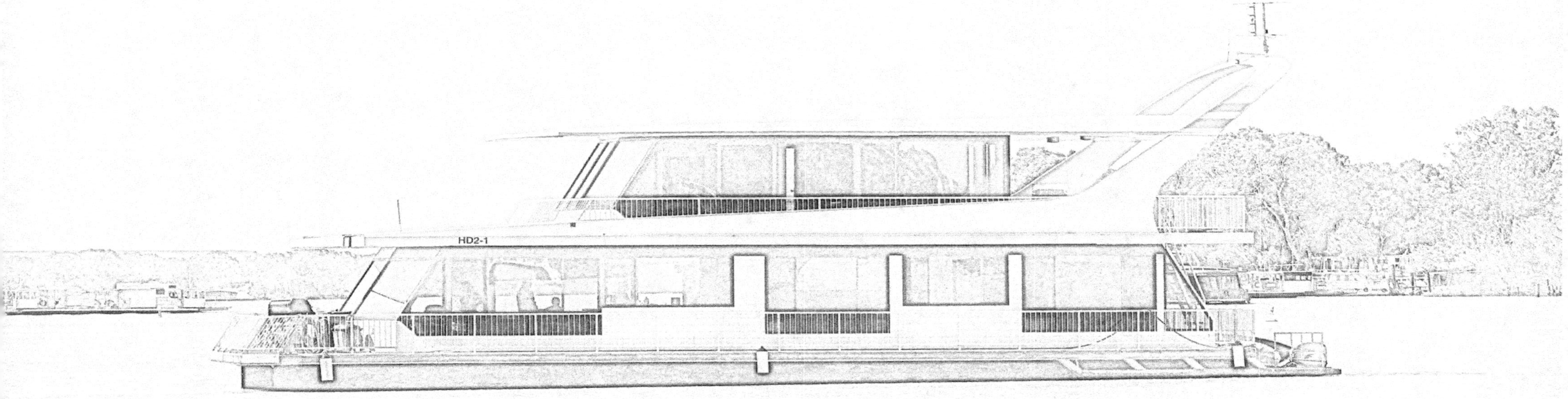
HD2-1

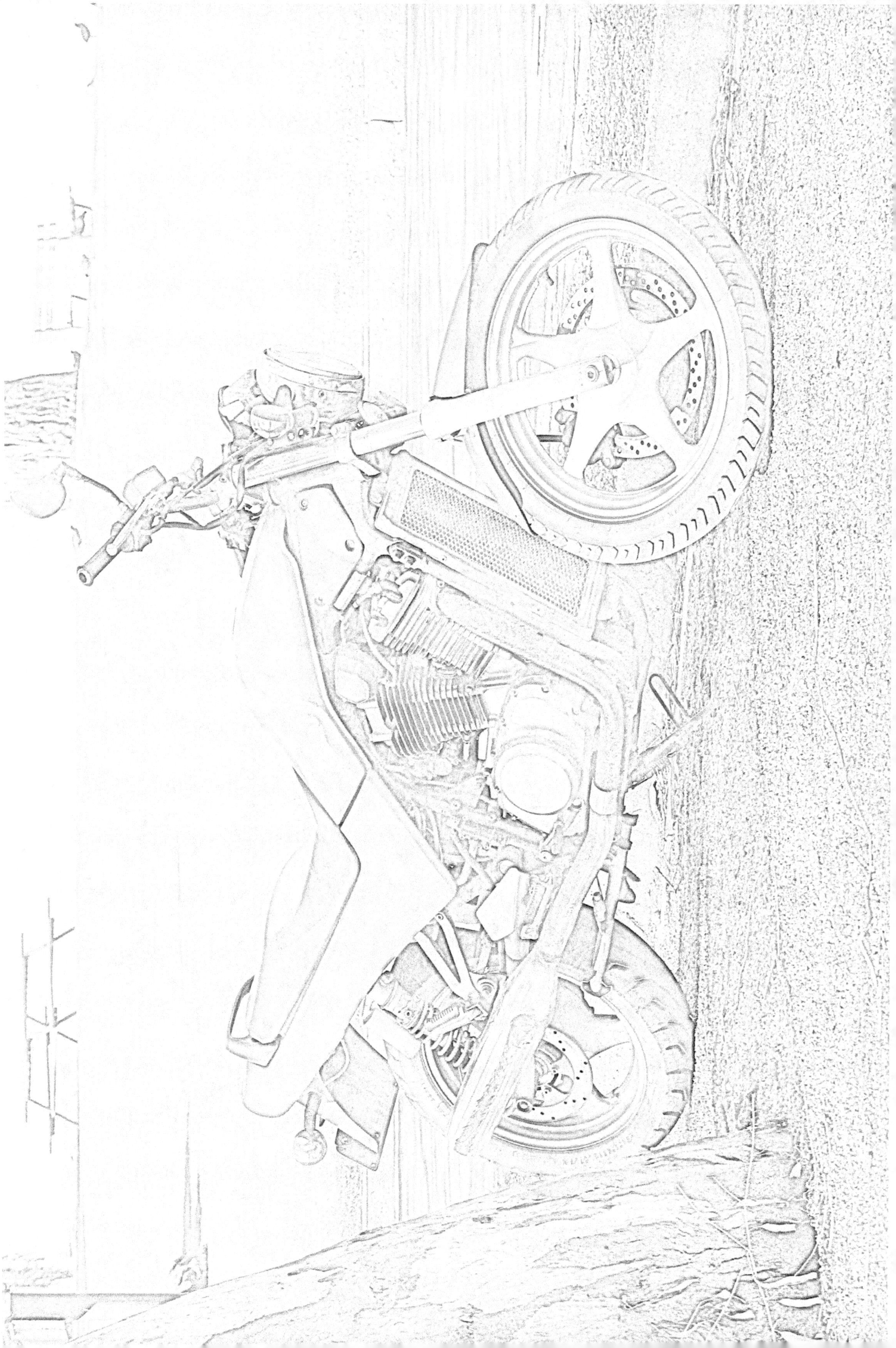

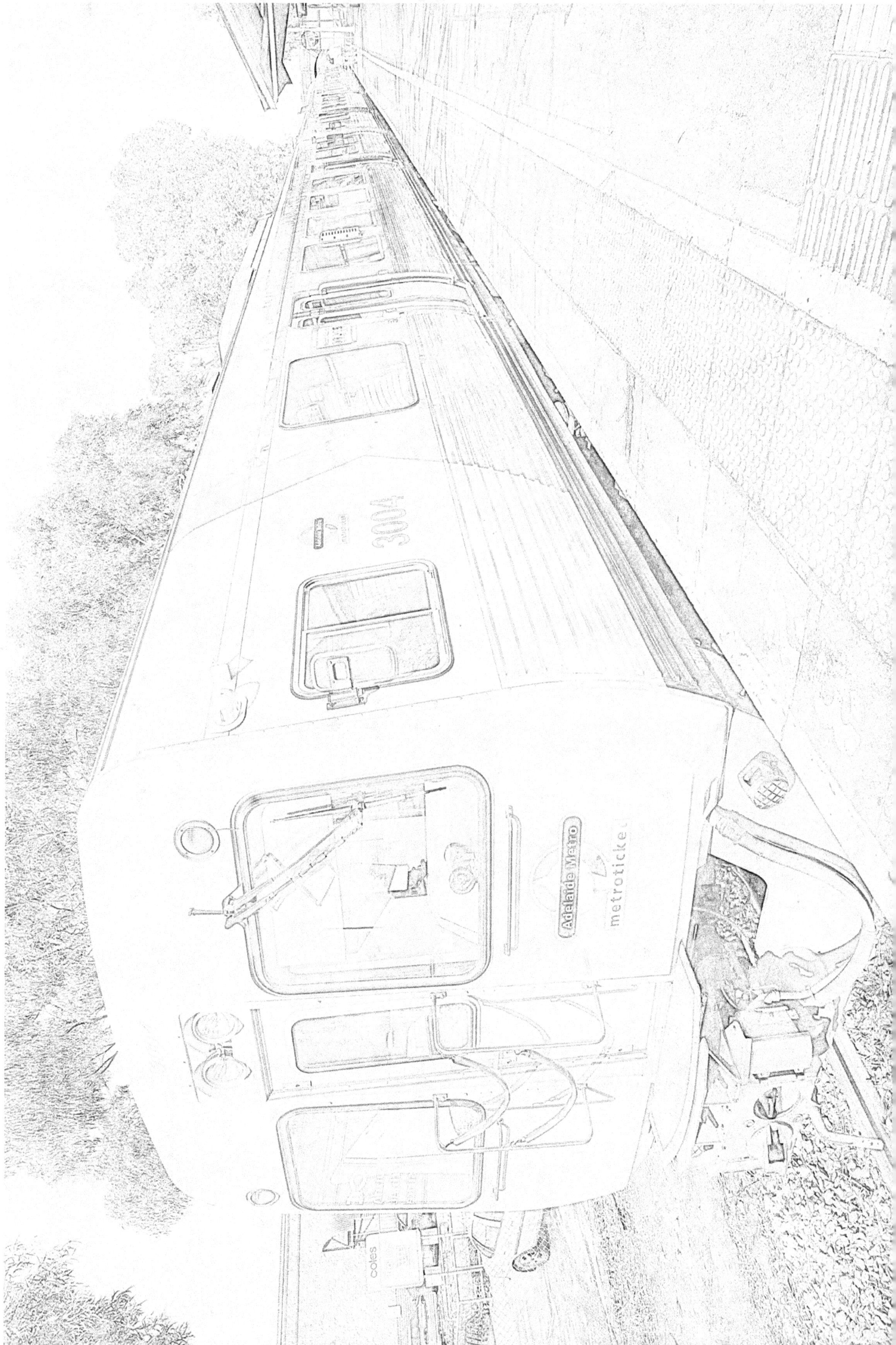

3004
Adelaide Metro
metroticket
coles

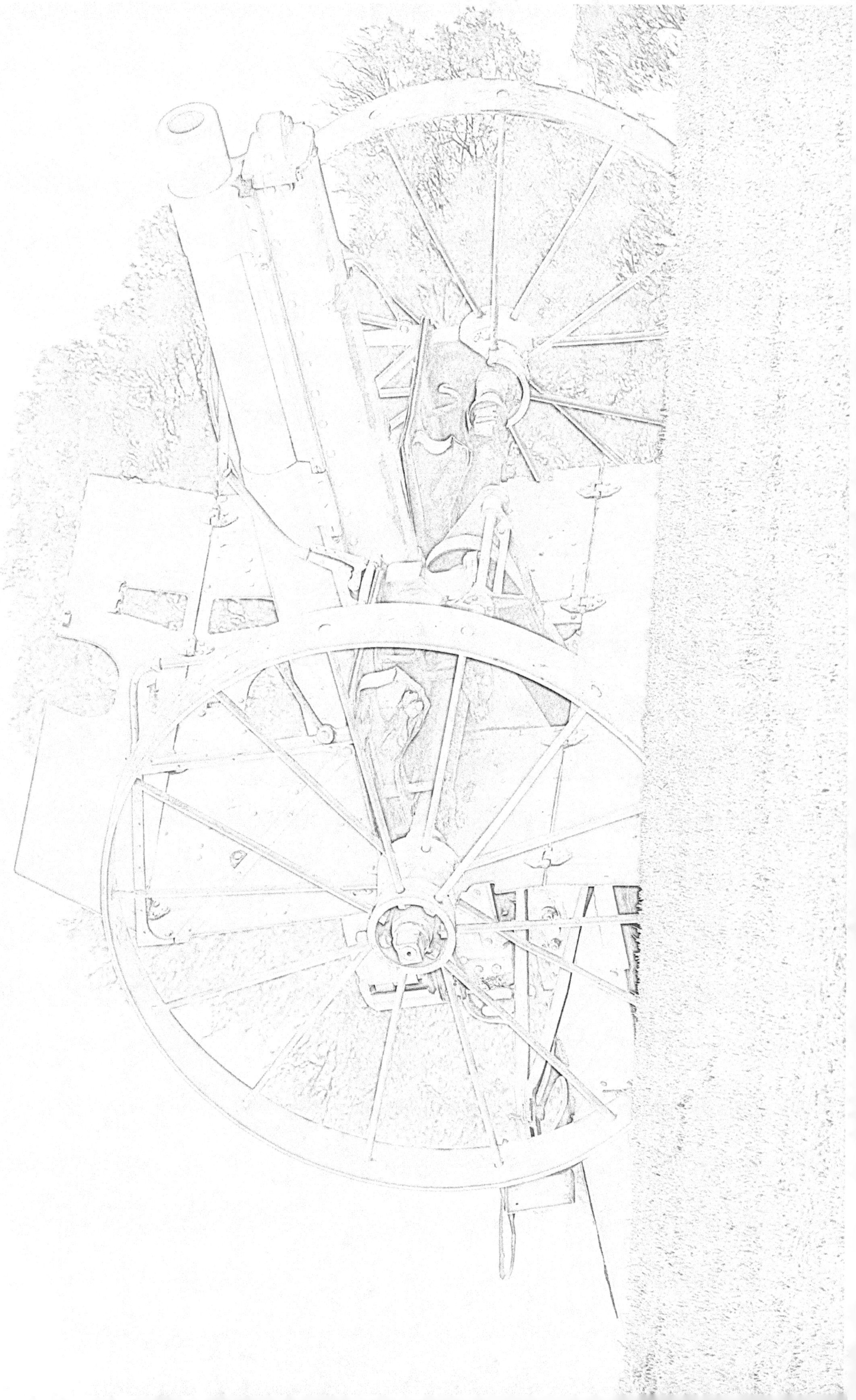

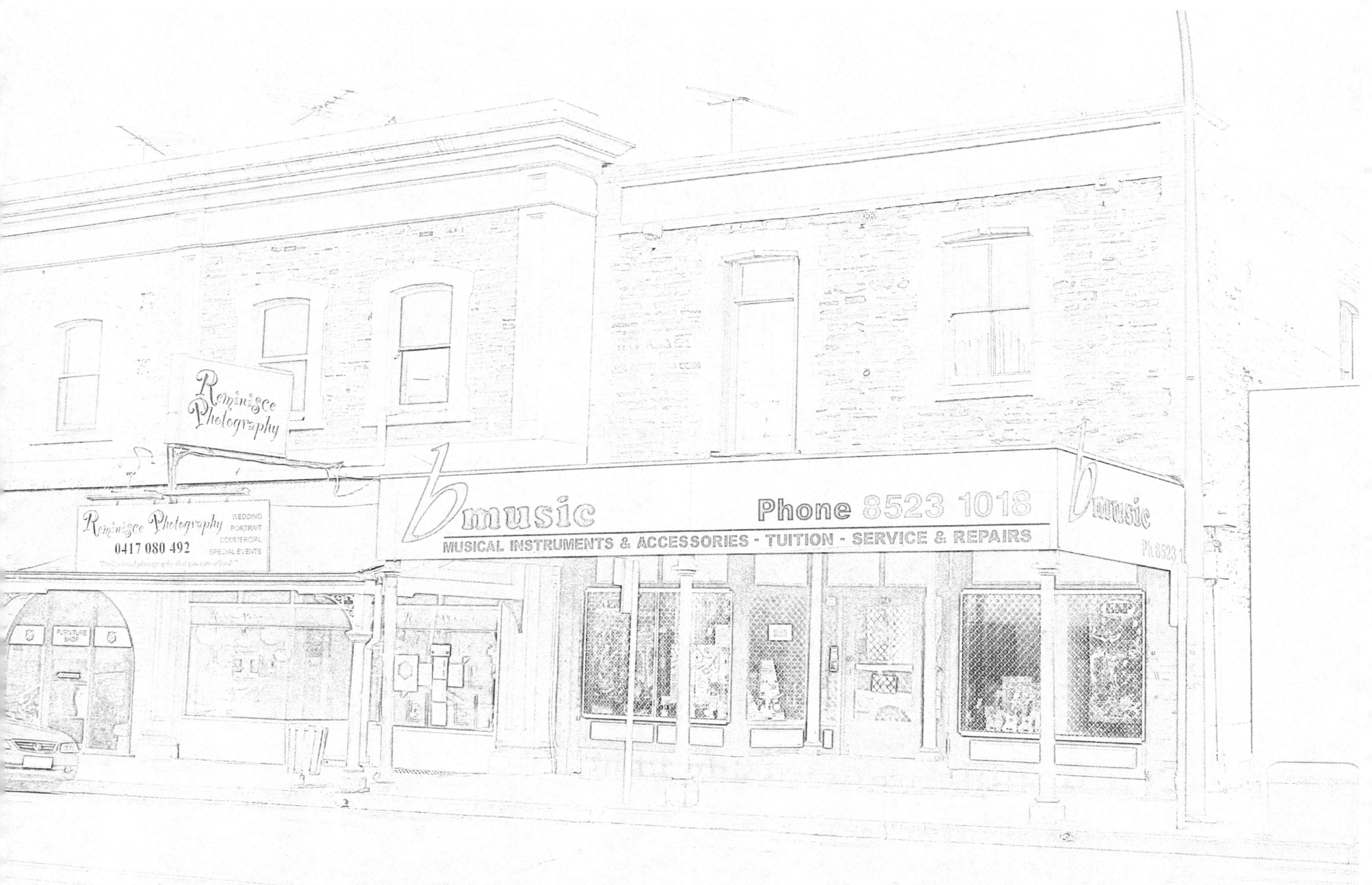
Reminisce Photography
Reminisce Photography
WEDDING
PORTRAIT
COMMERCIAL
SPECIAL EVENTS
0417 080 492
FURNITURE SHOP
bmusic
Phone 8523 1018
MUSICAL INSTRUMENTS & ACCESSORIES - TUITION - SERVICE & REPAIRS
bmusic

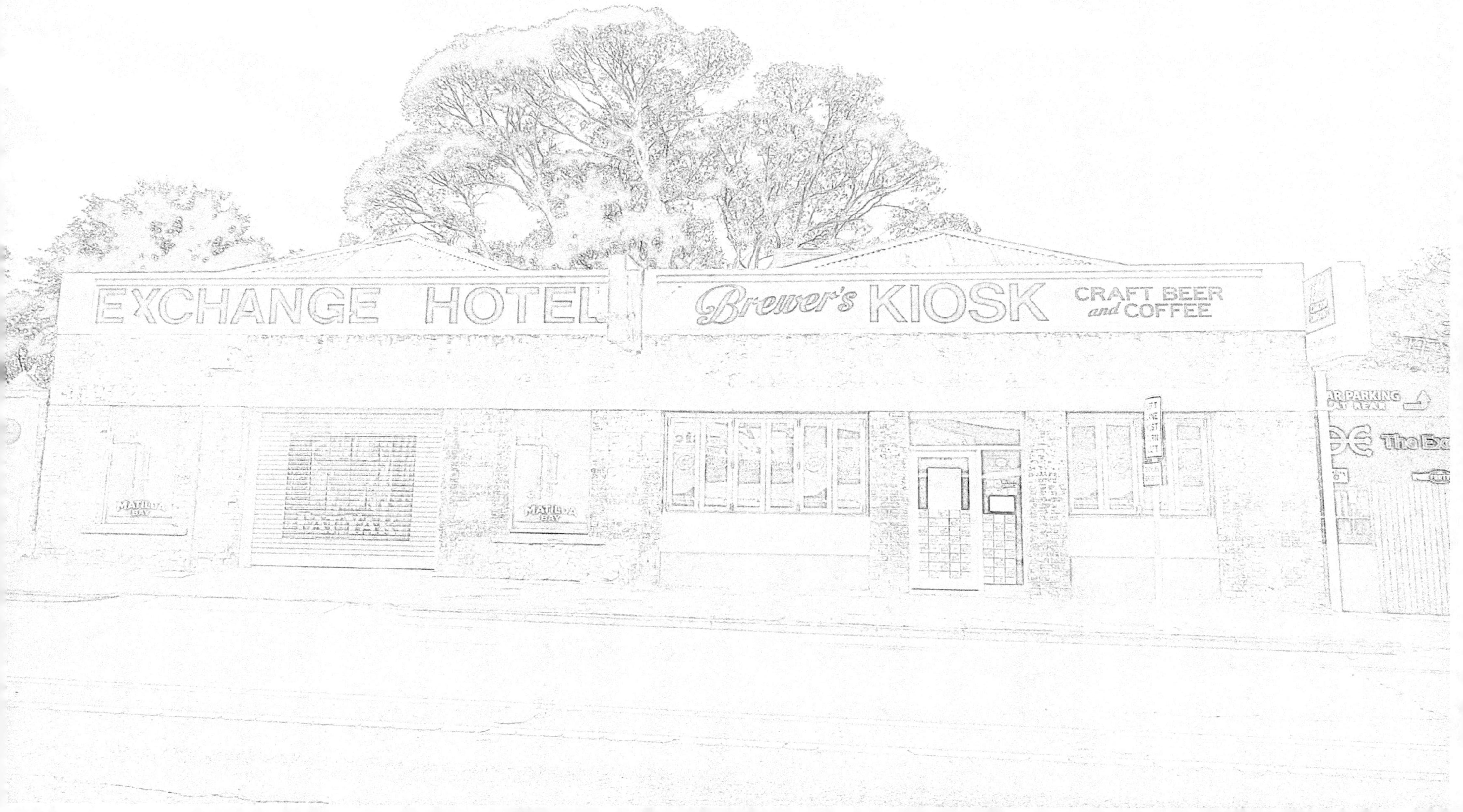
EXCHANGE HOTEL
Brewer's KIOSK
CRAFT BEER and COFFEE
MATILDA BAY
MATILDA BAY

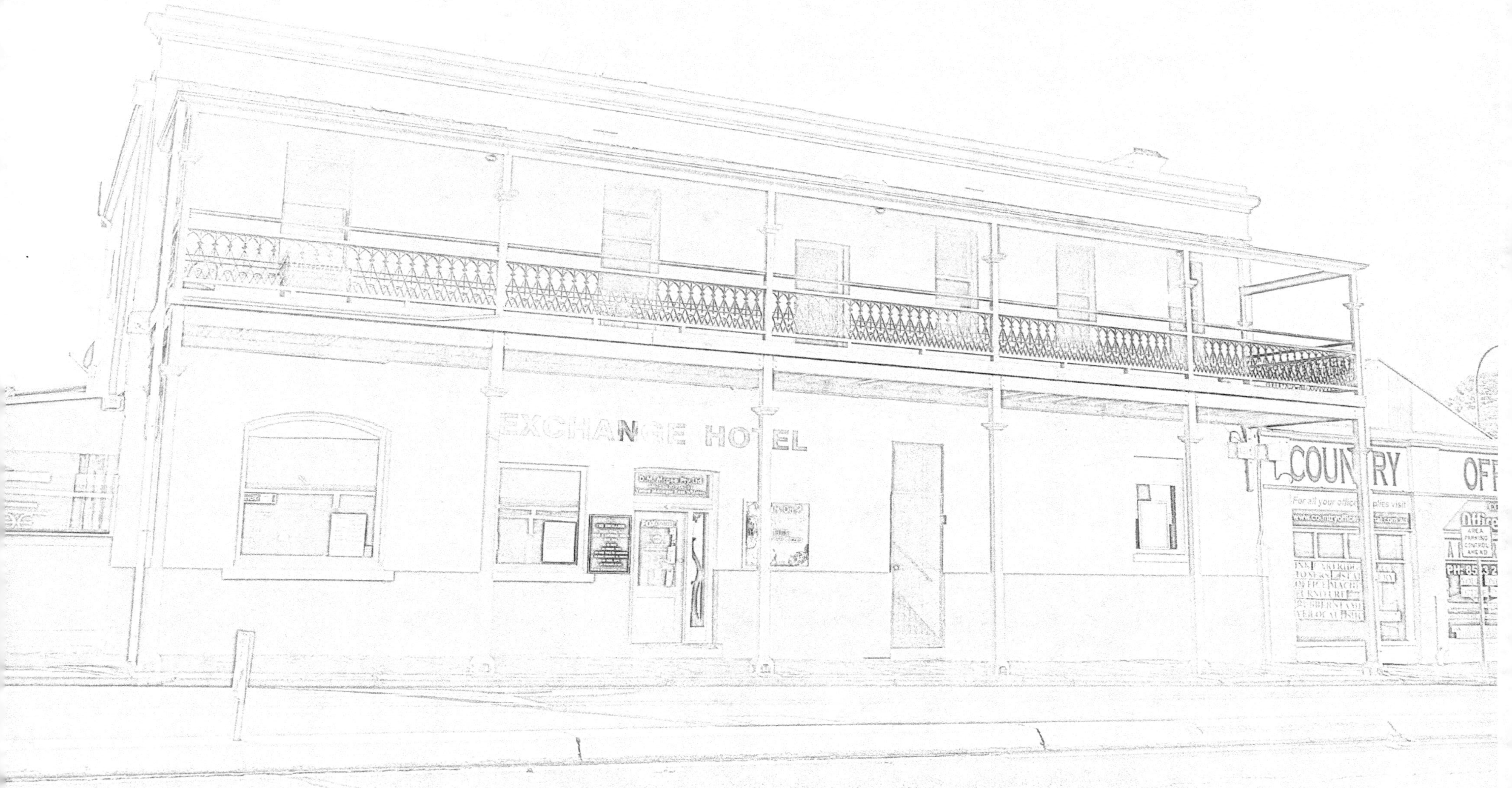
EXCHANGE HOTEL
COUN RY
For all your office plies visit

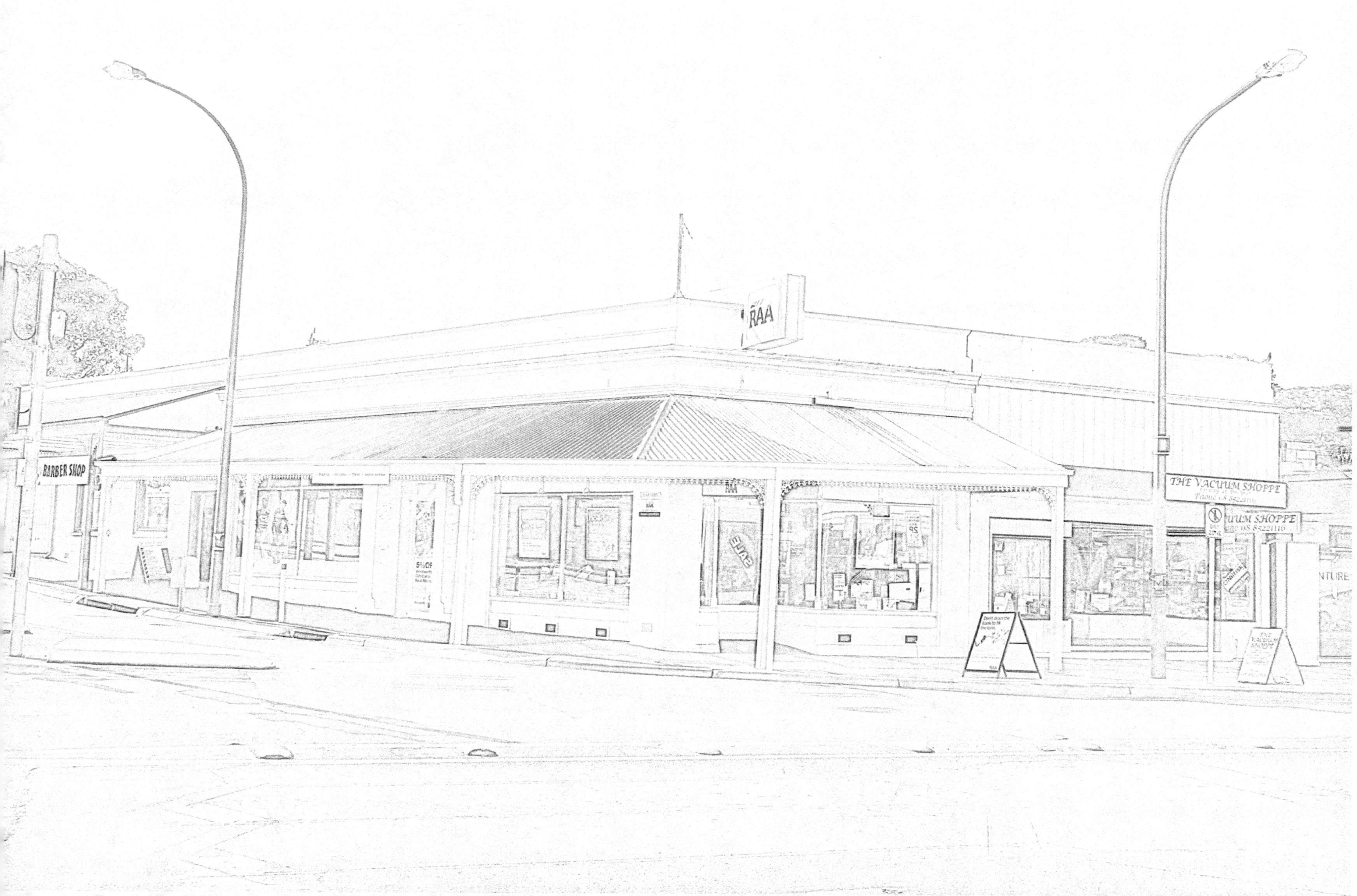
BARBER SHOP
RAA
SALE
THE VACUUM SHOPPE

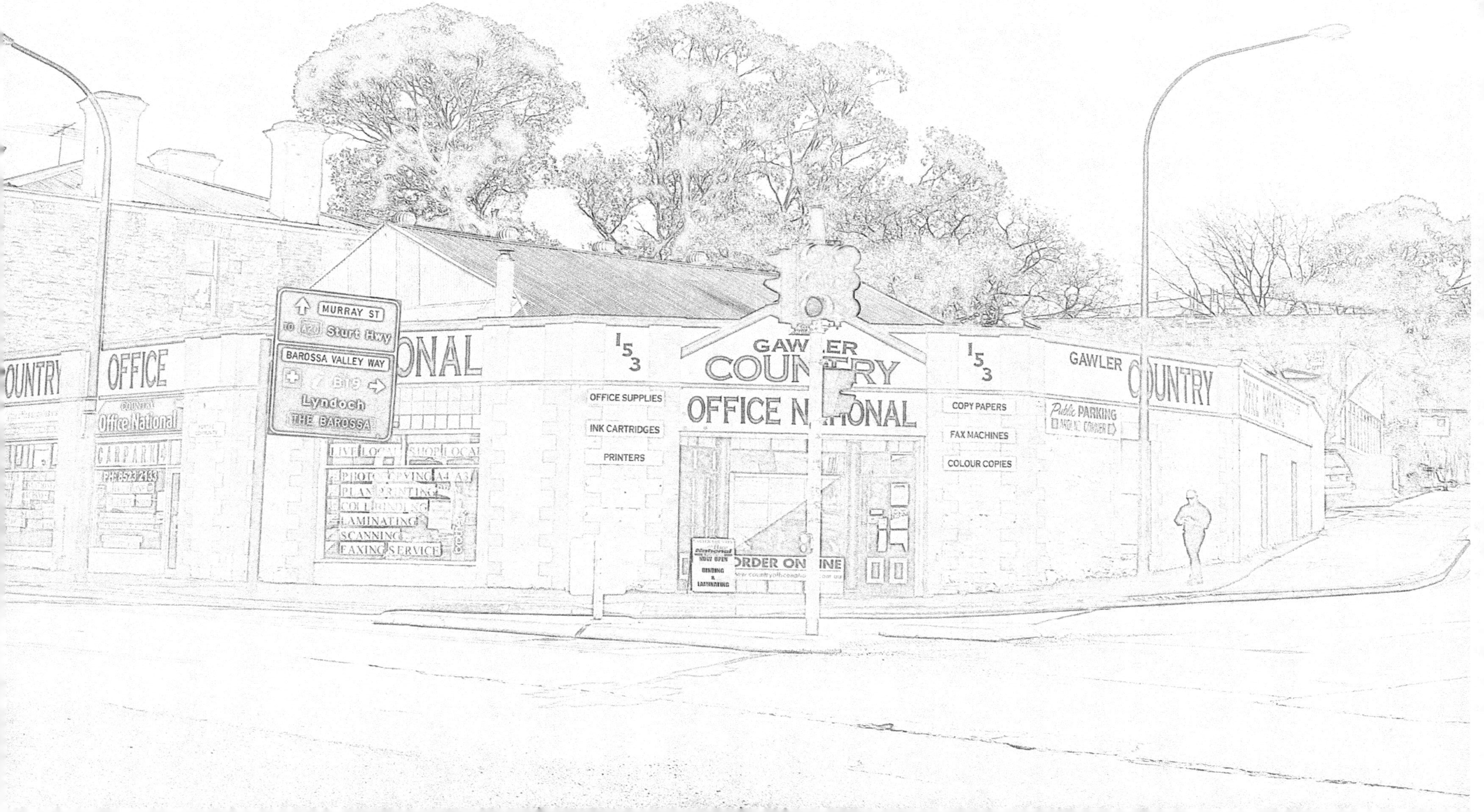
MURRAY ST
TO A20 Sturt Hwy
BAROSSA VALLEY WAY
B19
Lyndoch
THE BAROSSA
GAWLER
COUNTRY
OFFICE NATIONAL
153
OFFICE SUPPLIES
INK CARTRIDGES
PRINTERS
COPY PAPERS
FAX MACHINES
COLOUR COPIES
Public PARKING
OFFICE
Office National
CARPARK
PH: 8523 2133
LIVE LOCAL SHOP LOCAL
PLAN PRINTING
LAMINATING
SCANNING
FAXING SERVICE
ORDER ONLINE
NOW OPEN

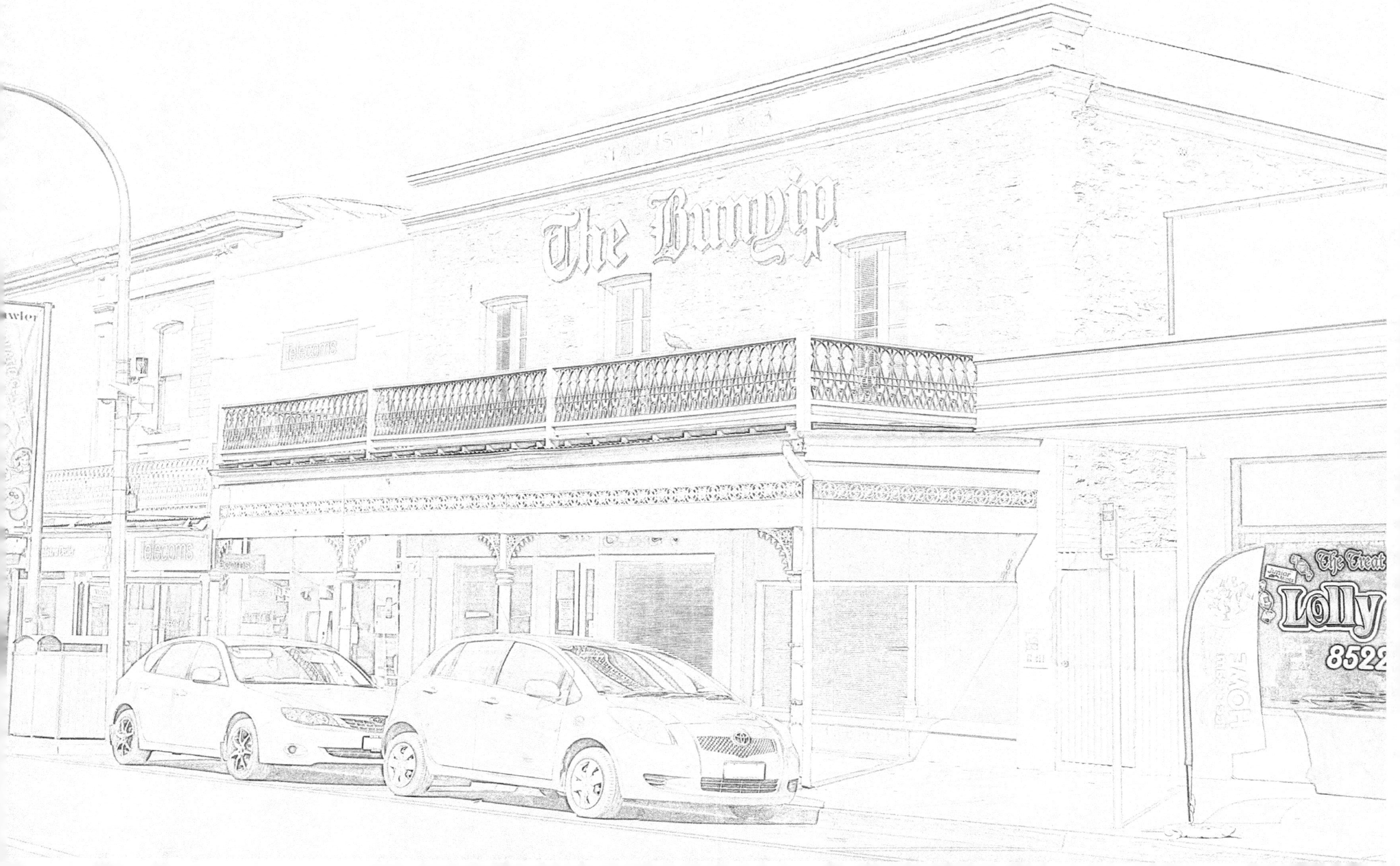
The Bunyip
Telecoms
Telecoms
The Great
Lolly
8522

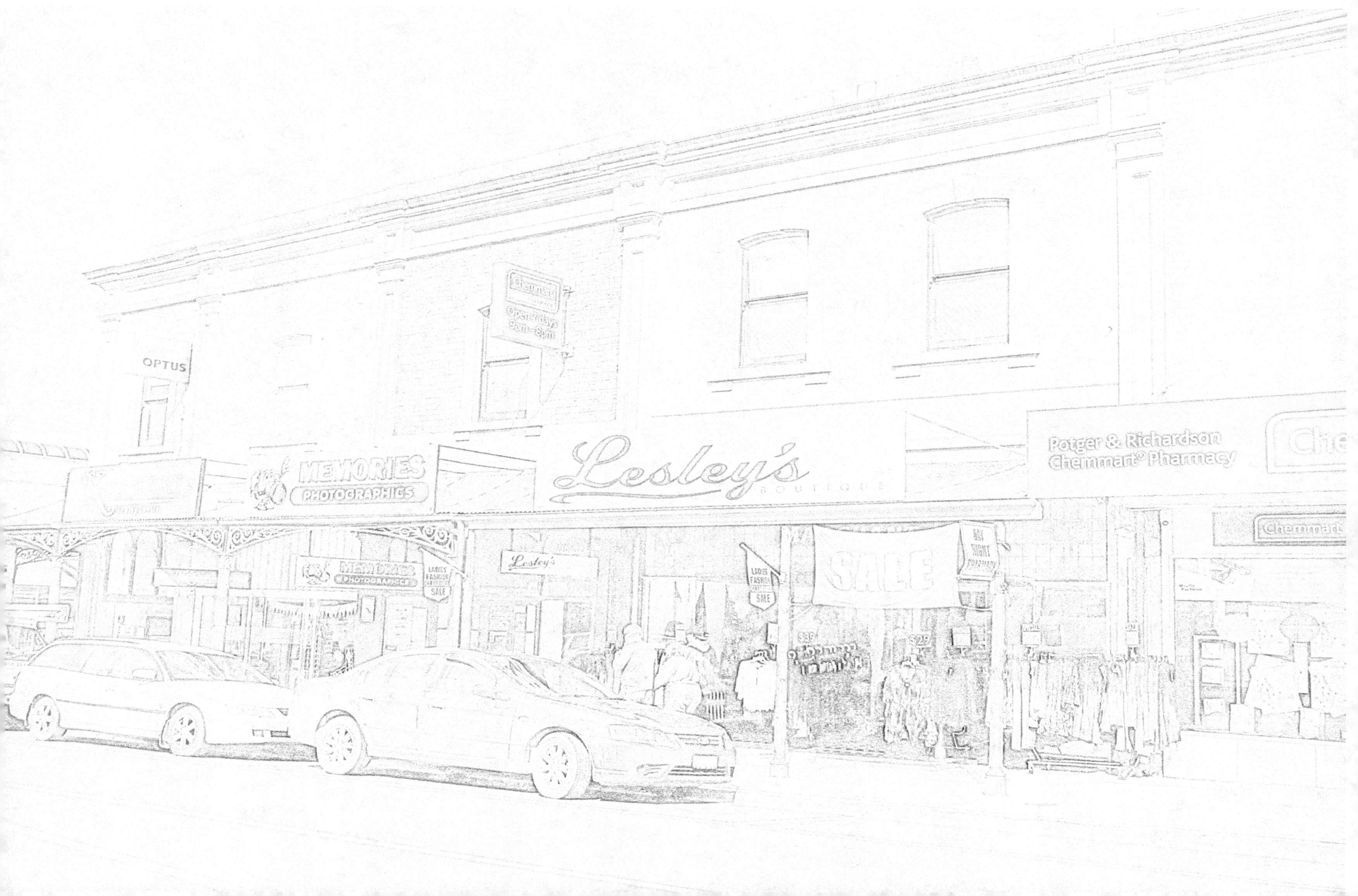
OPTUS
Opening days
9am - 8pm
MEMORIES
PHOTOGRAPHICS
Lesley's
BOUTIQUE
Potger & Richardson
Chemmart® Pharmacy
Lesley's
LADIES FASHION
SALE
SALE
$39
$29
Chemmart

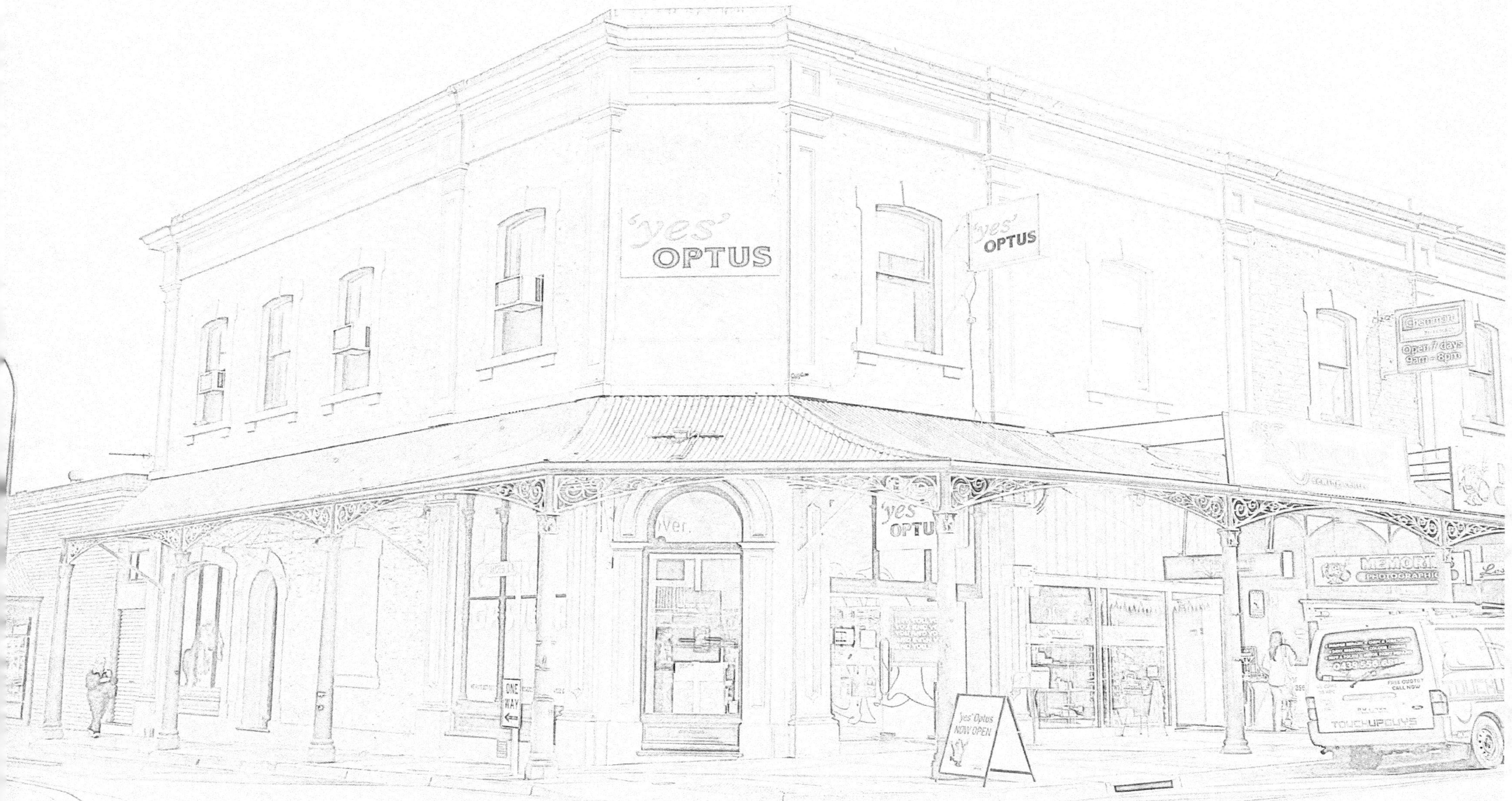
'yes' OPTUS
'yes' OPTUS
'yes' OPTUS
Open 7 days
9am - 8pm
ONE WAY
'yes' Optus
NOW OPEN
MEMORIES
PHOTOGRAPHIC
FREE QUOTE
CALL NOW
TOUCHUPGUYS

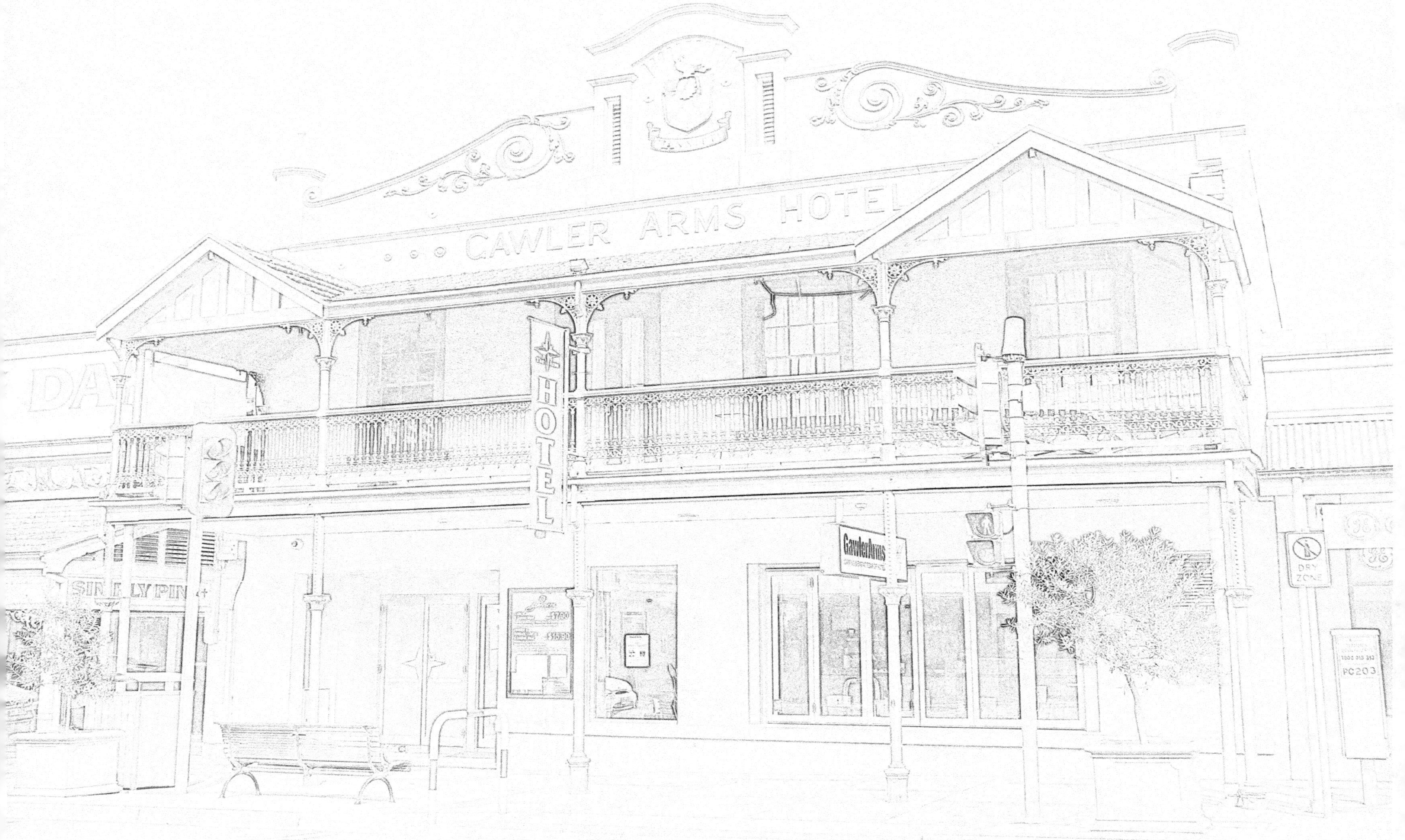
GAWLER ARMS HOTEL
HOTEL
GawlerArms
DRY ZONE
PC203

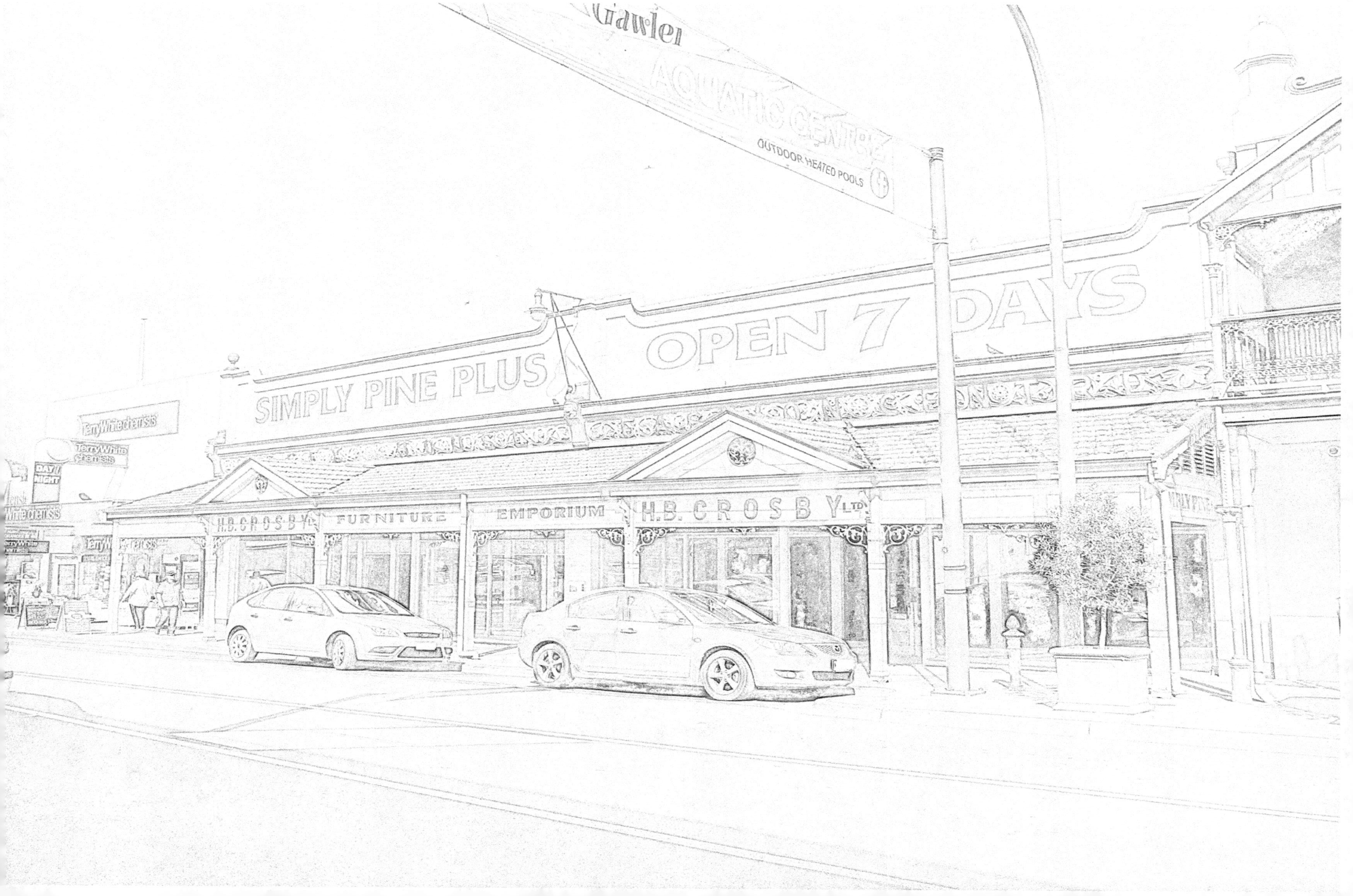
Gawler
AQUATIC CENTRE
OUTDOOR HEATED POOLS
SIMPLY PINE PLUS
OPEN 7 DAYS
H.B. CROSBY
FURNITURE
EMPORIUM
H.B. CROSBY LTD
TerryWhite chemists
DAY NIGHT

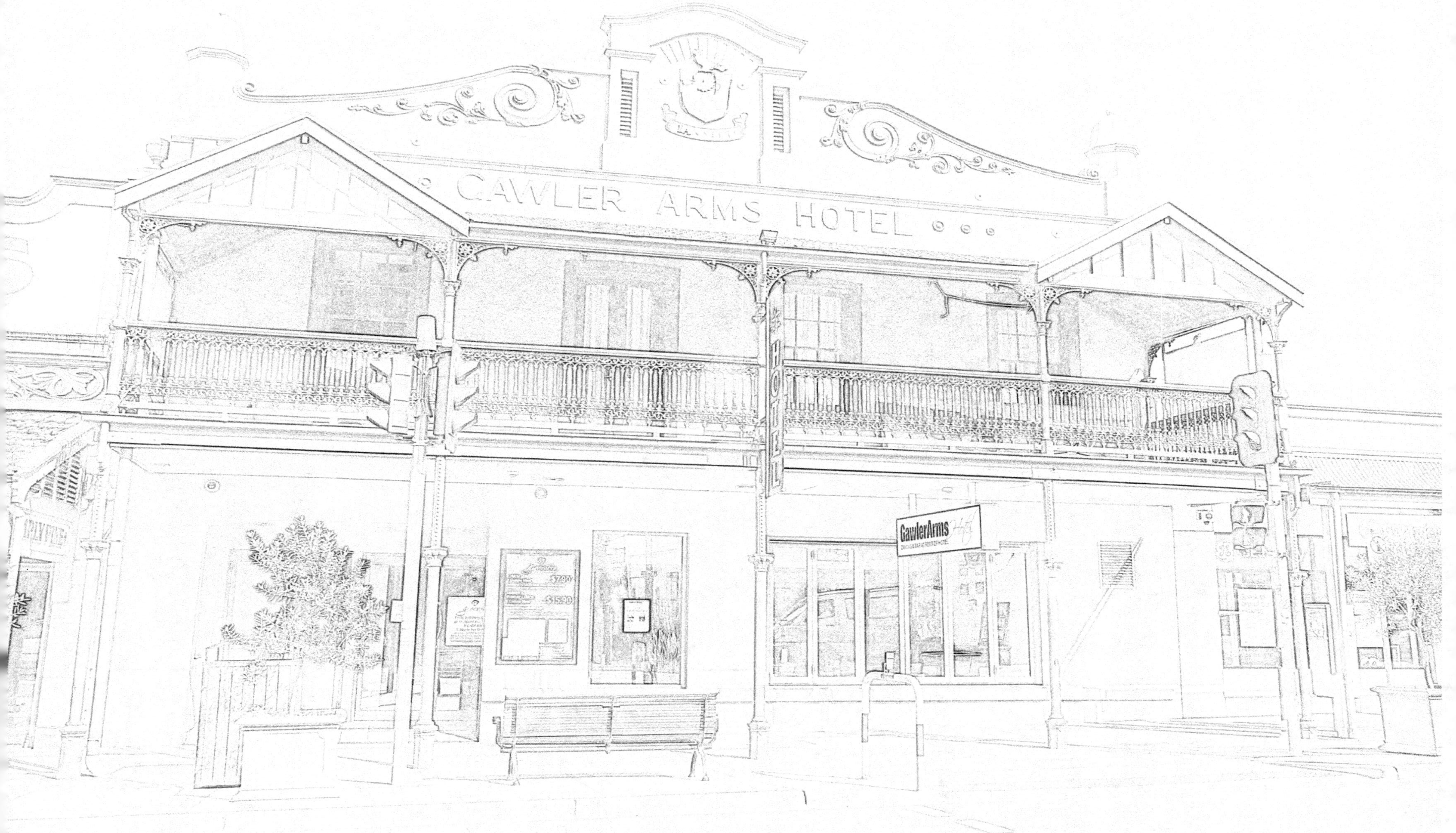
GAWLER ARMS HOTEL
HOTEL
GawlerArms

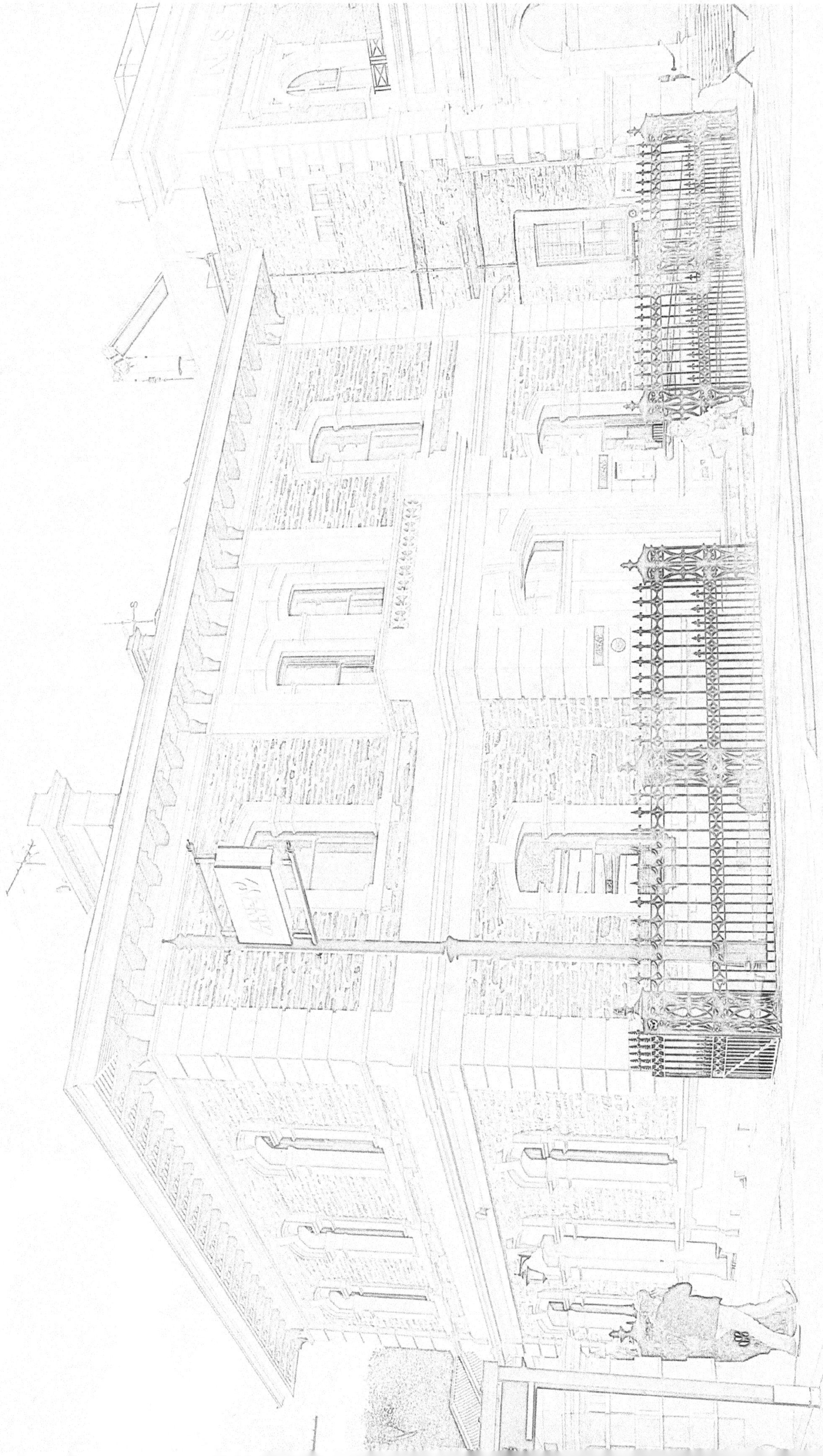

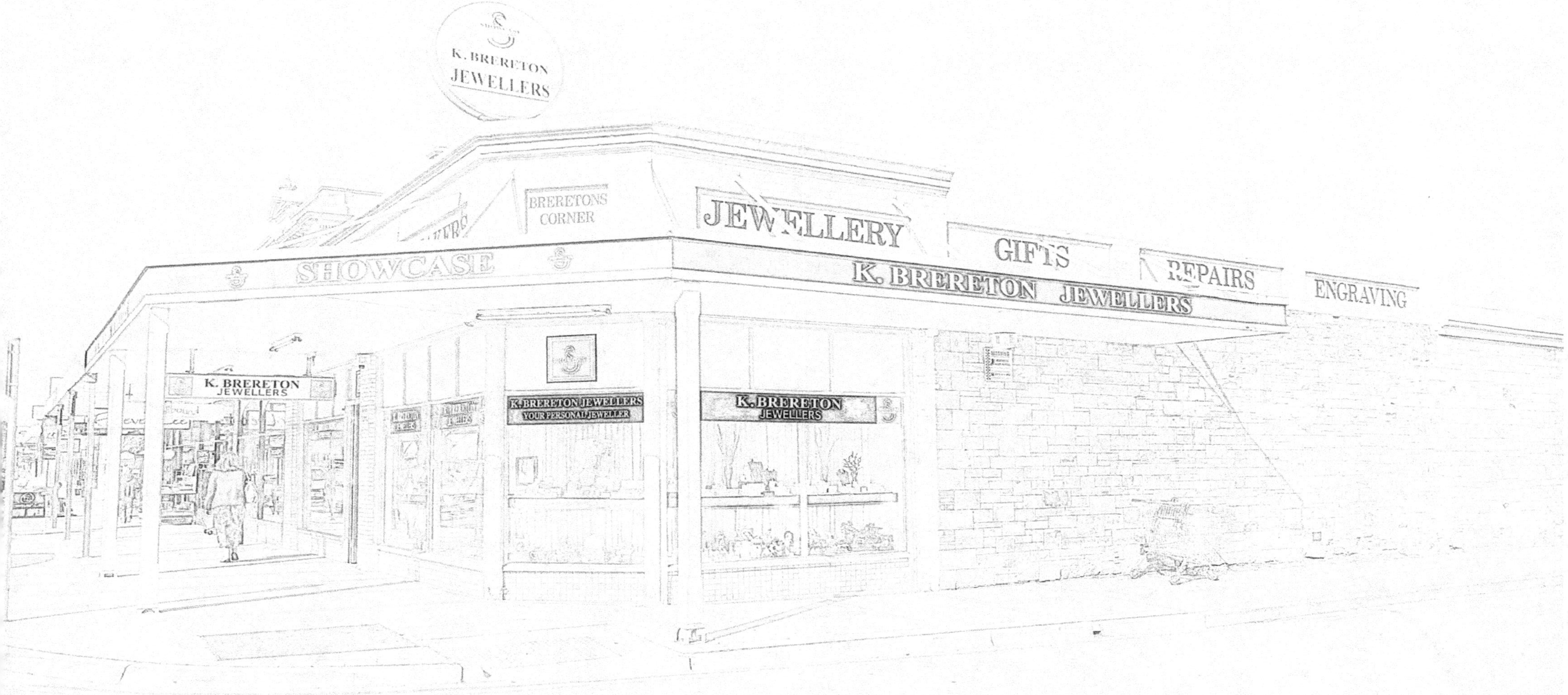
K. BRERETON
JEWELLERS
BRERETONS
CORNER
JEWELLERY
GIFTS
REPAIRS
ENGRAVING
SHOWCASE
K. BRERETON JEWELLERS
K. BRERETON
JEWELLERS
K. BRERETON JEWELLERS
YOUR PERSONAL JEWELLER
K. BRERETON
JEWELLERS

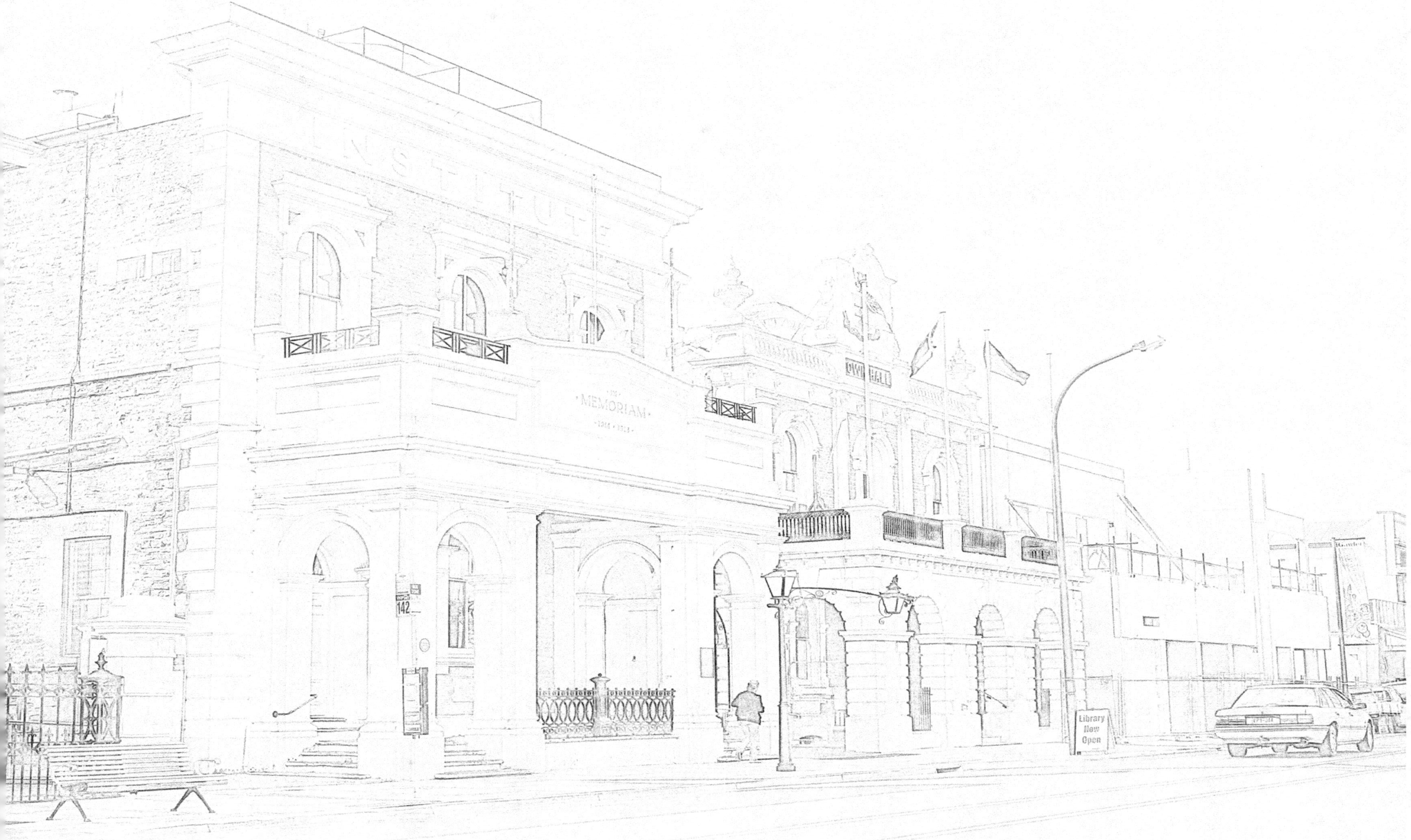
INSTITUTE
MEMORIAM
142
Library
Now
Open

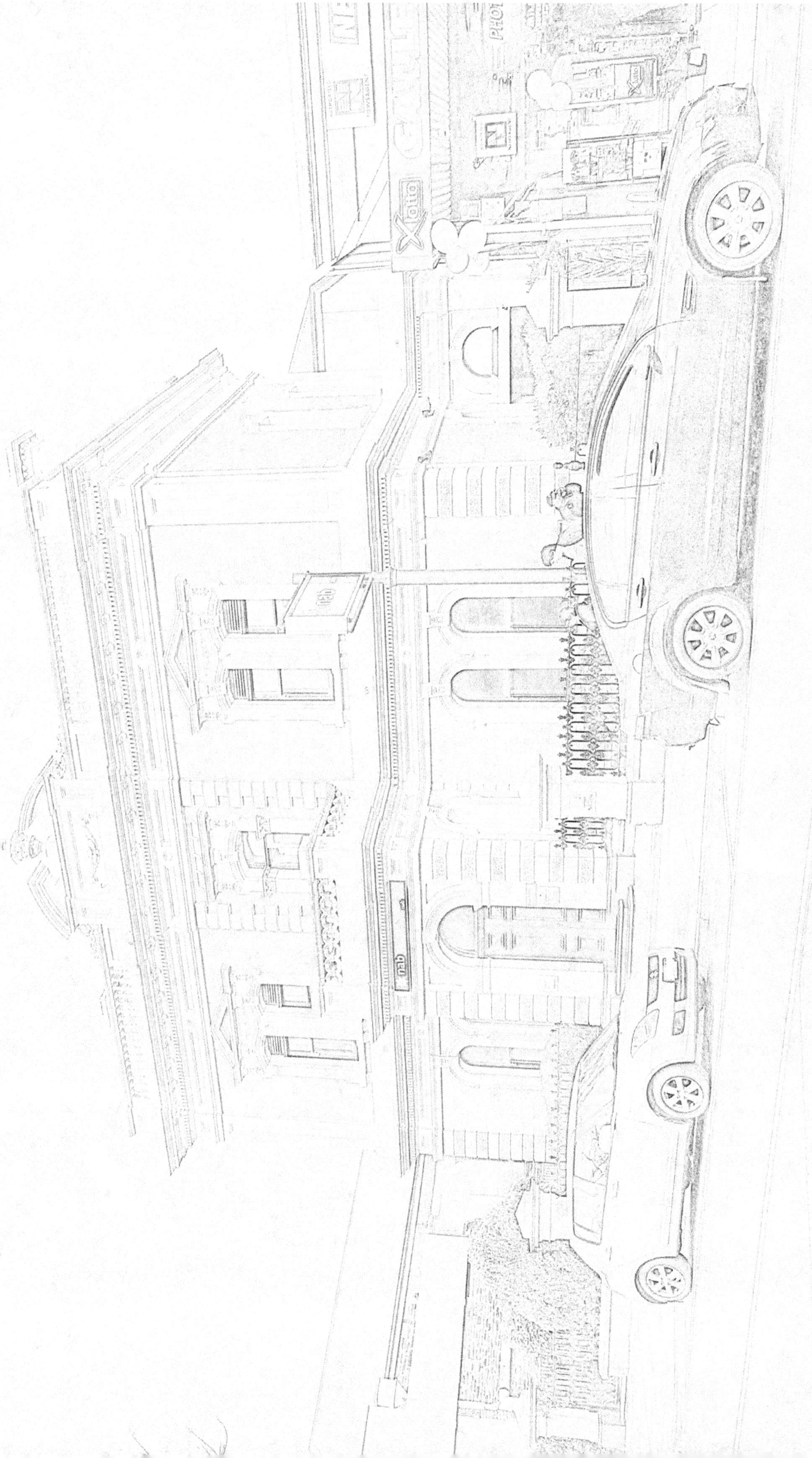
nab

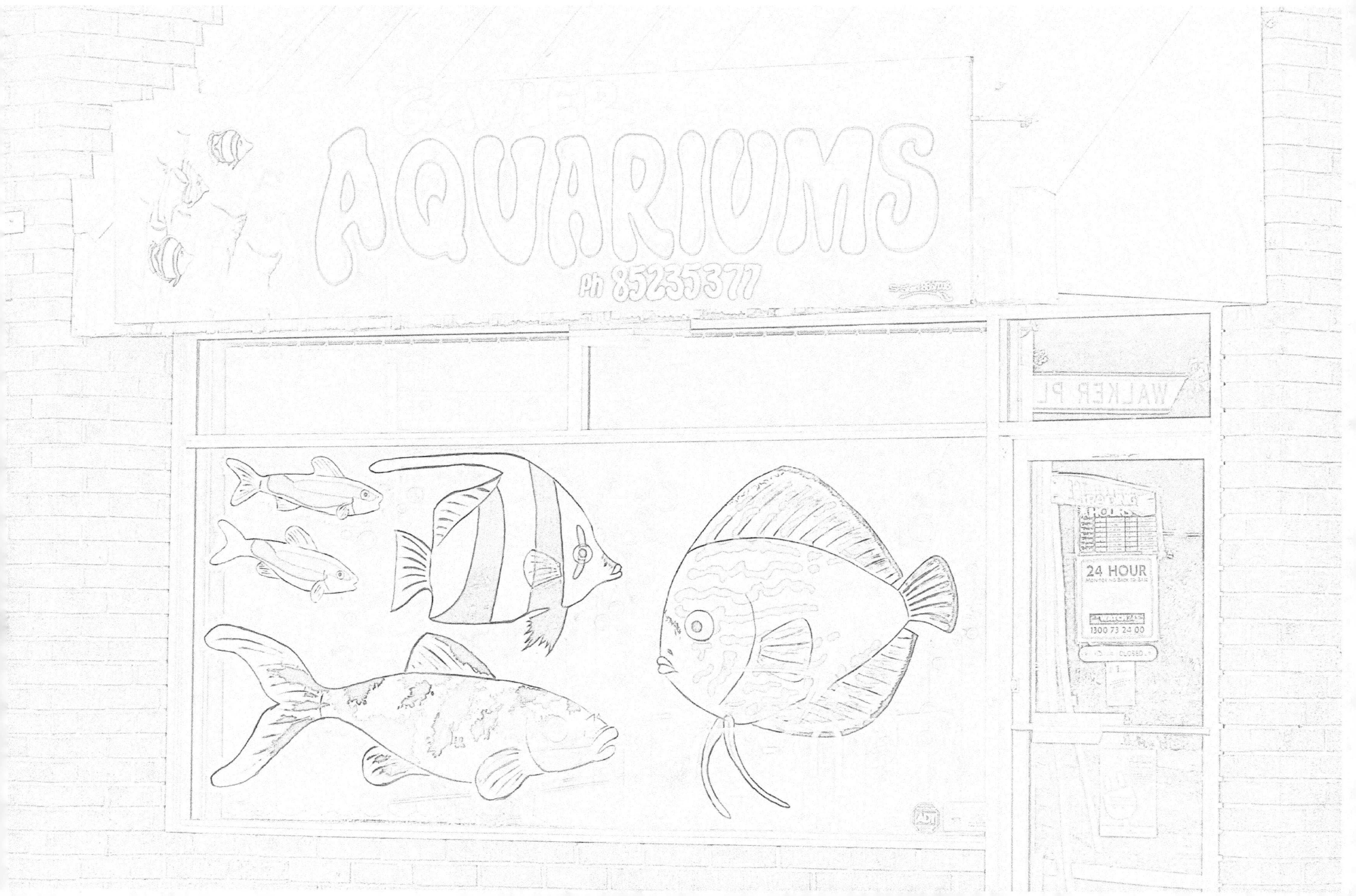
AQUARIUMS
Ph 85235377
WALKER PL
24 HOUR
1300 73 24 00
CLOSED

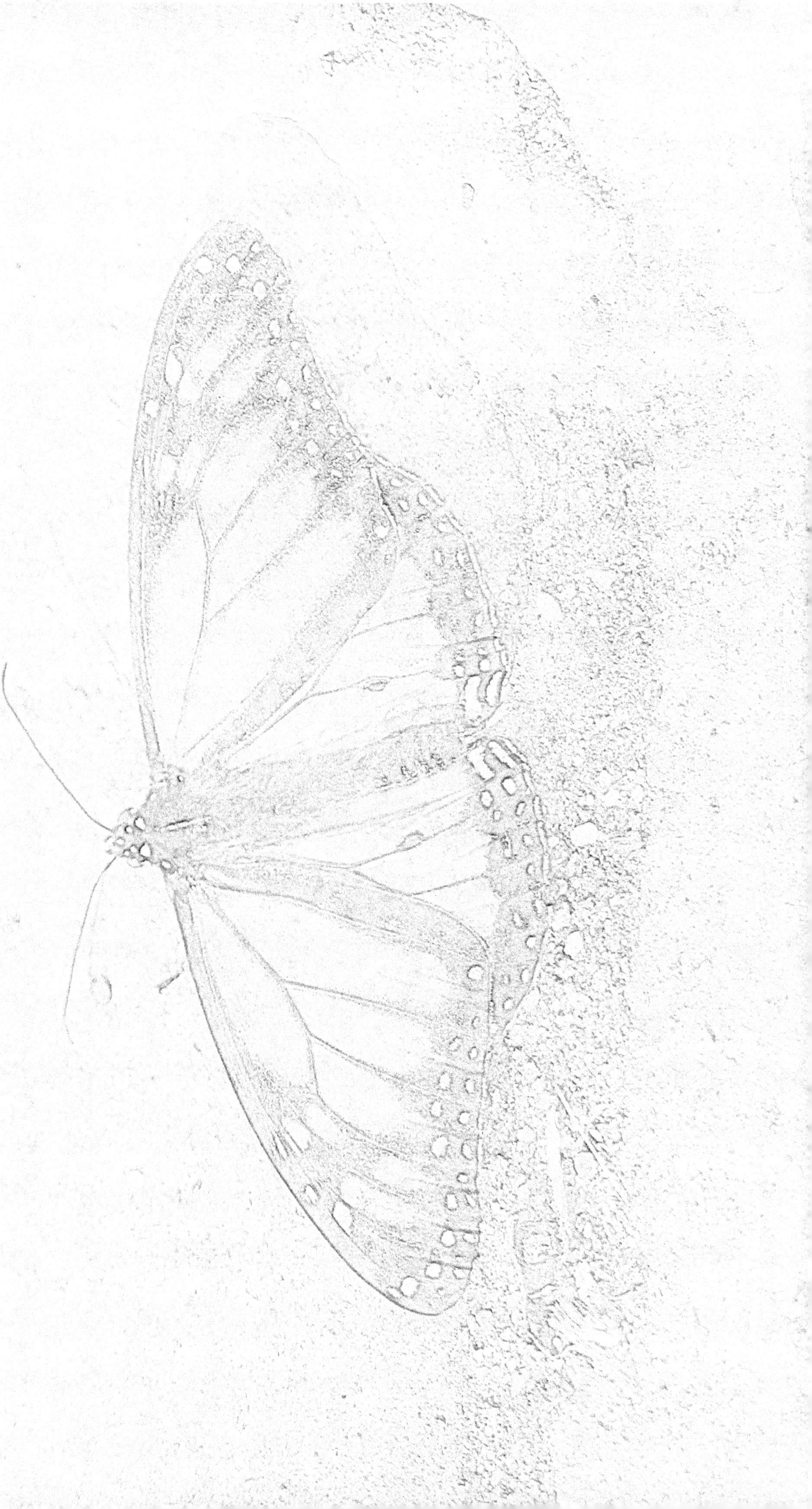

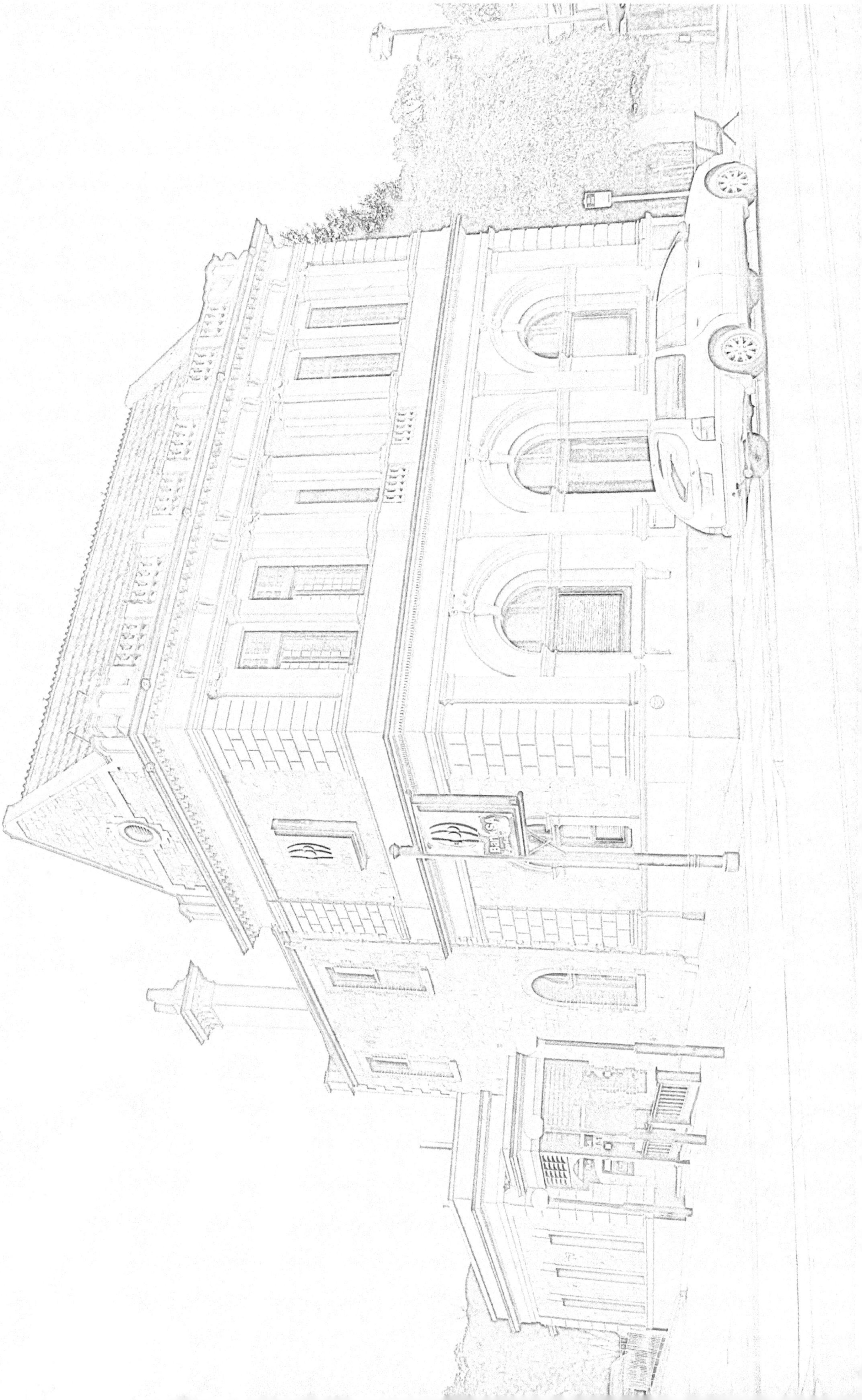

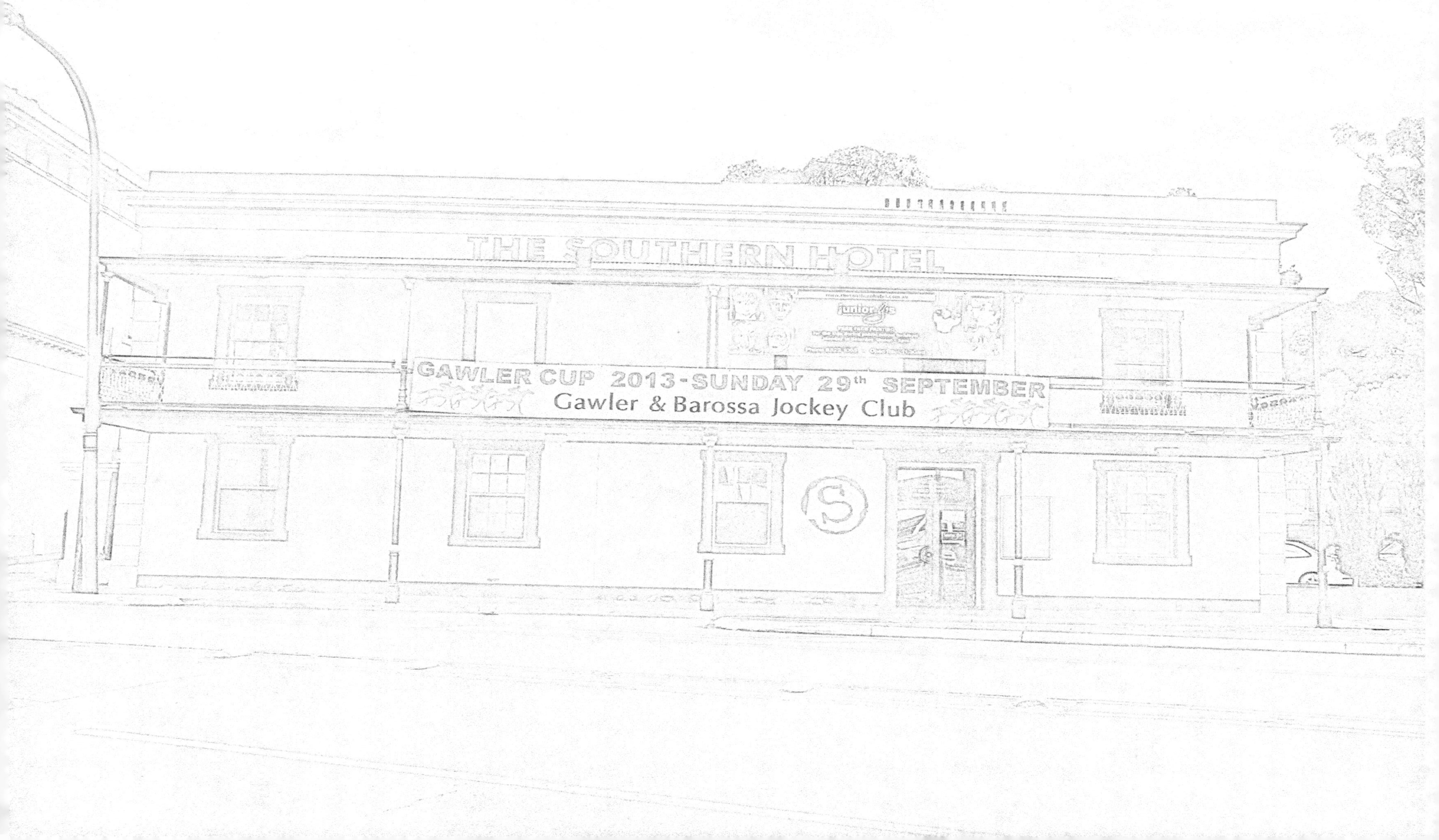
THE SOUTHERN HOTEL
GAWLER CUP 2013-SUNDAY 29th SEPTEMBER
Gawler & Barossa Jockey Club
S

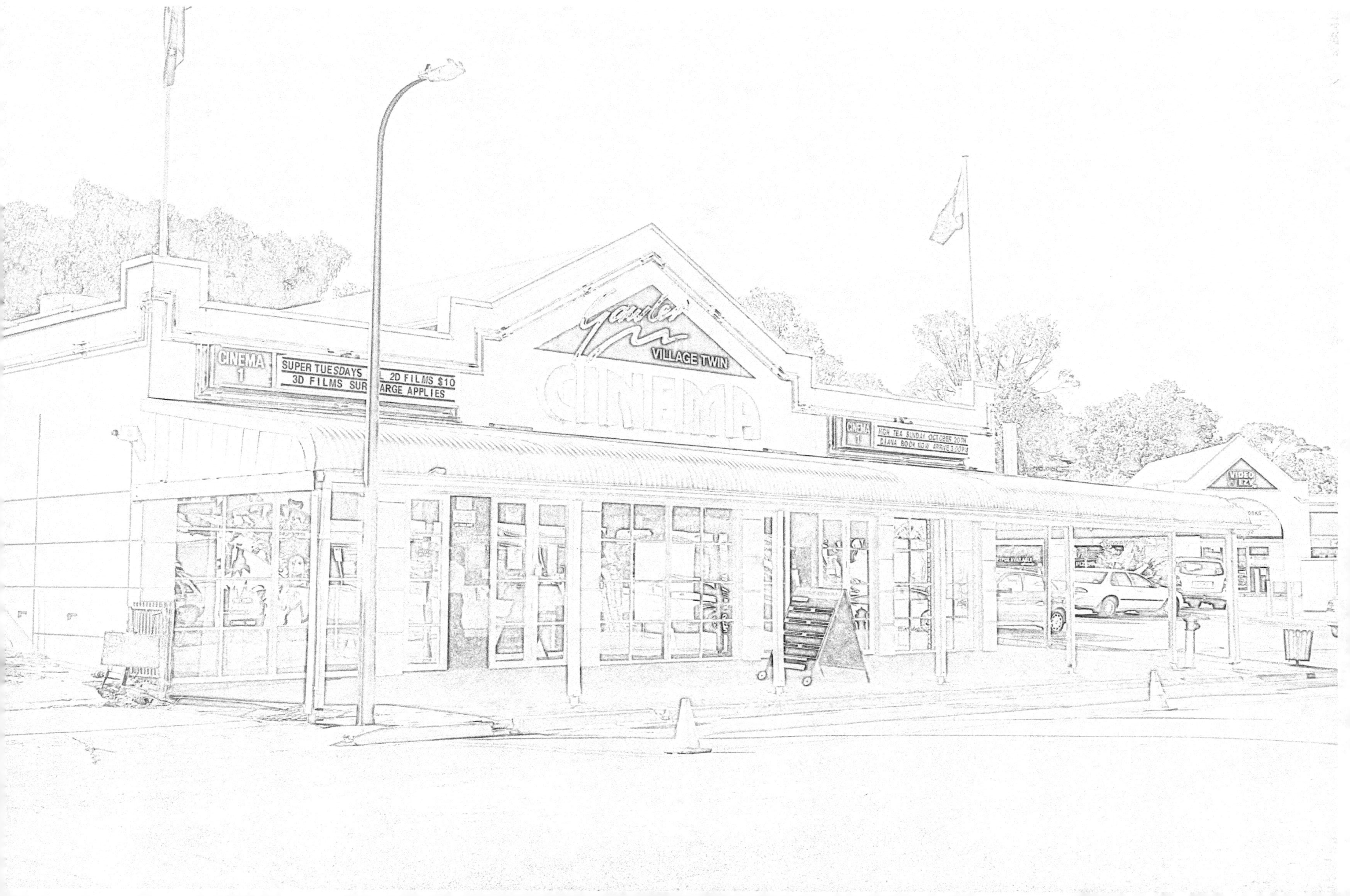
VILLAGE TWIN
CINEMA
CINEMA 1
SUPER TUESDAYS L 2D FILMS $10
3D FILMS SUR ARGE APPLIES
CINEMA 1
HIGH TEA SUNDAY OCTOBER 20TH

La Dolce Vita

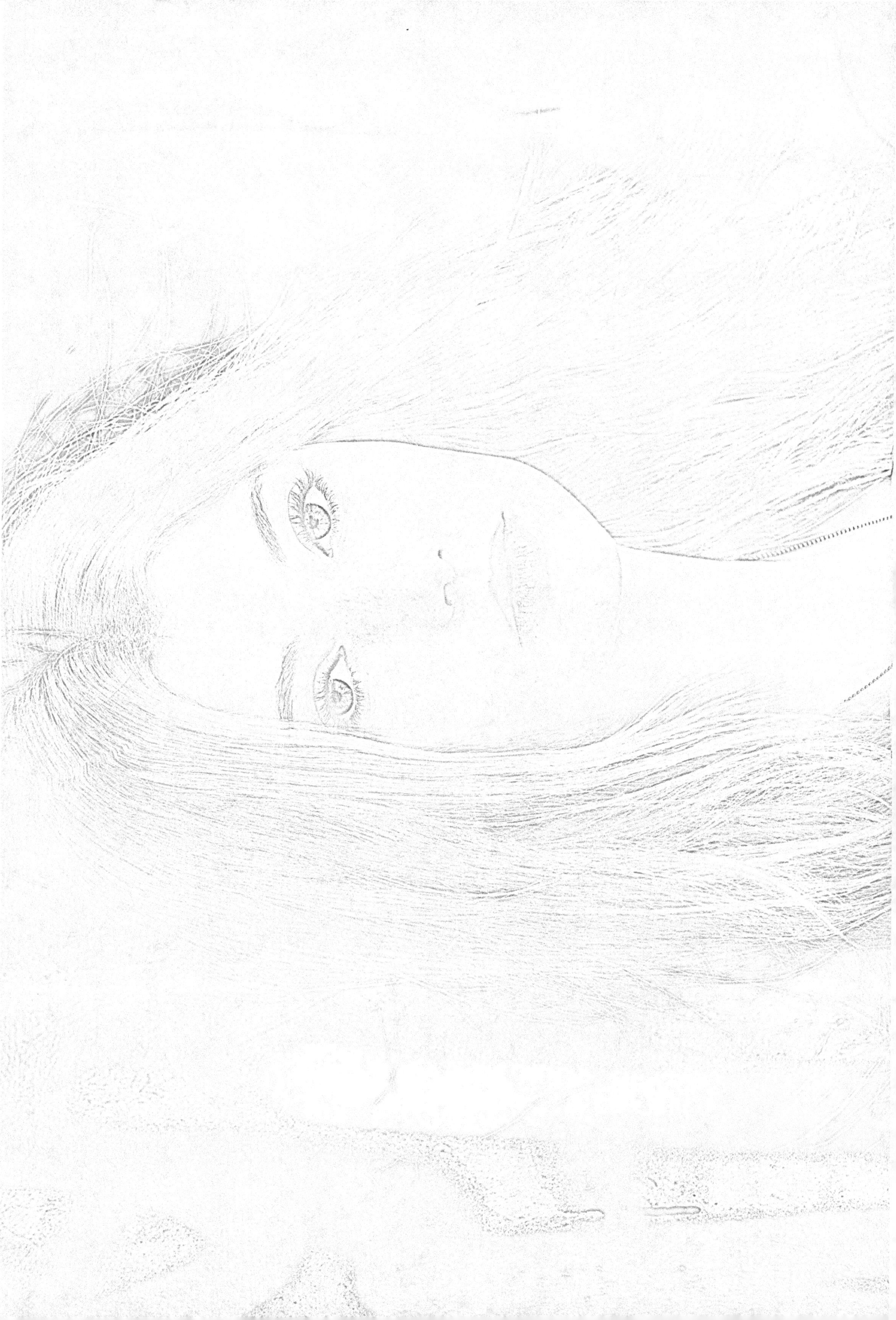

www.ingramcontent.com/pod-product-compliance
Lightning Source LLC
Chambersburg PA
CBHW081058180526
45170CB00005B/1803